The IDEA MAGAZINE FOR TEACHERS® MAILBOX®

2008–2009 YEARBOOK

The Education Center, Inc.
Greensboro, North Carolina

The Mailbox® 2008–2009 Preschool Yearbook

Managing Editor, *The Mailbox* Magazine: Kimberly Brugger-Murphy

Editorial Team: Becky S. Andrews, Diane Badden, Kimberley Bruck, Karen A. Brudnak, Pam Crane, Sarah Foreman, Pierce Foster, Margaret Freed (COVER ARTIST), Tazmen Hansen, Marsha Heim, Lori Z. Henry, Kitty Lowrance, Brenda Miner, Jennifer Nunn, Tina Petersen, Mark Rainey, Greg D. Rieves, Hope Rodgers, Eliseo De Jesus Santos II, Rebecca Saunders, Donna K. Teal, Rachael Traylor, Sharon M. Tresino, Zane Williard

ISBN10 1-56234-920-1
ISBN13 978-156234-920-2
ISSN 1088-5536

Printed in the United States of America.

The Education Center, Inc.
P.O. Box 9753
Greensboro, NC 27429-0753

Look for *The Mailbox® 2009–2010 Preschool Yearbook* in the summer of 2010. The Education Center, Inc., is the publisher of *The Mailbox®*, *Teacher's Helper®*, and *Learning®* magazines, as well as other fine products. Look for these wherever quality teacher materials are sold, call 1-800-714-7991, or visit www.themailbox.com.

Contents

Arts & Crafts for Little Hands

Arts & Crafts for Little Hands

Not-So-Smooth Apple

Put a spin on traditional apple art with this idea! Tint a bowl of sand with red food coloring (or obtain red sand from a craft store). Then add red glitter to the sand. Brush the surface of a small white paper plate with glue; then sprinkle the sand and glitter mixture over the glue. After the project is dry, attach a construction paper stem and leaf to the plate to complete the apple.

Fran Chupper
Lil Sprouts Preschool
Toms River, NJ

Terrific Kitchen Tools!

Gather a variety of kitchen tools, such as a potato masher, a spatula, a whisk, and a meat-tenderizing mallet. Place each kitchen tool next to a shallow container of tempera paint. Dip a tool in the corresponding paint and then press or roll it on a sheet of construction paper or newsprint. Continue in the same manner with the remaining kitchen tools and containers of paint until a desired effect is achieved.

Mary Bauer
St. Mary's Early Education Program
Hockessin, DE

Hidden Colors

To make this simple artwork, use bright-colored crayons to scribble on a sheet of white construction paper. Then use a small paint roller to spread black paint over the paper. While the paint is wet, use a craft stick to draw in the paint. The craft stick removes the black paint so the white paper and crayon marks show through. The result is a lovely piece of artwork with a unique effect!

Marla Gartenberg
Silver Spring Learning Center
Silver Spring, MD

Press, Paint, Pull

This artwork gives the artist a fine-motor workout! Press pieces of painter's tape onto a sheet of finger-paint paper. Repeat the process until a desired effect is achieved. Then fingerpaint the entire surface of the paper with a variety of colors. When the paint is dry, remove the tape from the paper to reveal the hidden design. Simply lovely!

Tracey Mikos
Celebration Baptist Preschool
Tallahassee, FL

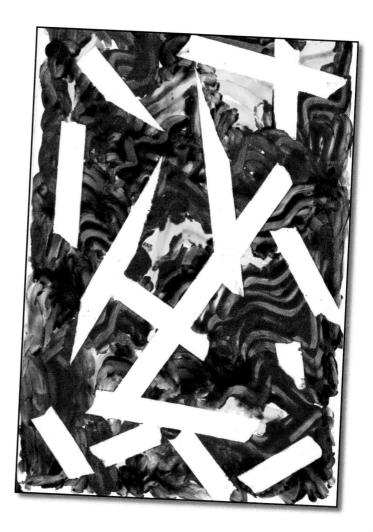

Arts & Crafts for Little Hands

Rubber Band Art

Try this fun idea for a twist on traditional string art! Cut several large rubber bands in half; then grasp each rubber band piece with a spring-style clothespin. Tape each clothespin closed. Simply drag the loose end of a rubber band through a shallow container of paint and then drag, tap, or swirl it around on a sheet of paper. Apply more paint as needed. If desired, mount this creative artwork on a contrasting sheet of construction paper.

Polly Skinn
East Hills Moravian Church Nursery School
Bethlehem, PA

Dazzling Decoupage

Preserve a little bit of nature with a shimmering shine! In advance, collect a variety of natural items, such as leaves, twigs, and pinecones. Also obtain decoupage medium from a local craft store. To begin, paint the entire surface of a natural item with tempera paint; then set it aside to dry. After the paint is dry, brush a coat of decoupage over the entire item; then allow it to dry to a dazzling finish!

Ann Zelter and Jenny Knoll
Salem Lutheran Preschool
Springville, NY

One-of-a-Kind Tree

Try this nifty idea for making a unique fall tree! To begin, cut out a brown construction paper tree and attach it to a sheet of construction paper. Next, cut a variety of red, orange, yellow, and brown pictures from old magazines. Glue the pictures to the tree to create fun fall foliage.

Beth Baranowski
Roselle Park, NJ

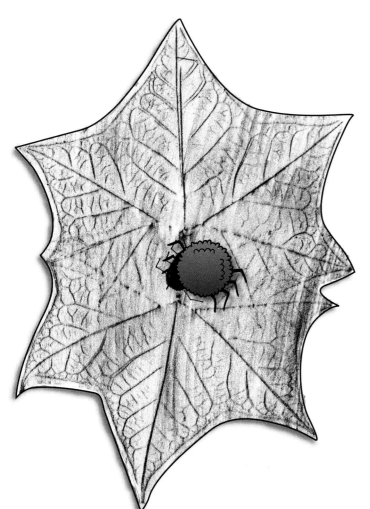

Spectacular Spiderweb!

Mother Nature lends a hand in creating these awesome spiderwebs! Tape two large leaves, similar in shape and size, to a tabletop so they resemble a spiderweb. Place a sheet of white paper on top of the leaves. Next, use the side of an unwrapped black crayon to rub across the paper. Then cut around the leaf rubbing to create a spiderweb shape. Finally, glue a pom-pom to the resulting web to make a spider's body. Use a marker to draw the spider's legs.

Angie Zerinsky
Fort Scott, KS

Arts & Crafts for Little Hands

It's Frosty!

This simple art activity captures that frosty winter feeling! Use a white crayon to draw a winter scene on a sheet of black or dark blue construction paper. Then use a cotton swab or a small paintbrush to paint over the scene with a solution of epsom salt dissolved in warm water. The result is a lovely, wintry piece of artwork.

Melissa Rose
Early Childhood Alliance
Fort Wayne, IN

A Special Tree

Glue green-tinted penne noodles to a tree cutout. Next, squeeze a mixture of white paint and glue onto the tree; then sprinkle mini pom-poms and sequins over the mixture. To complete the project, mount a headshot photograph on a star cutout and attach it to the top of the tree.

Dana Stout
Tarpey Elementary
Clovis, CA

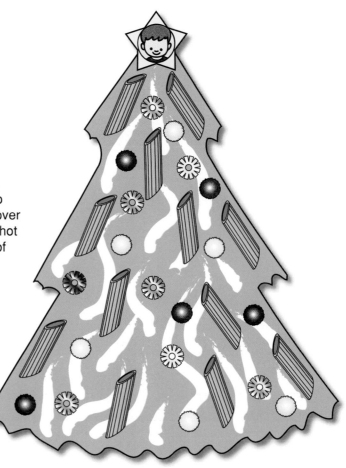

Syrup Slide

The result of this simple process art is a colorful masterpiece. Slightly dilute several containers of white corn syrup. Then tint the syrup with neon food coloring. Use spoons to drizzle the corn syrup onto a sheet of waxed paper. Next, place a light-colored sheet of construction paper over the waxed paper and then drag it across the waxed paper. Allow the resulting artwork to dry for several days.

C. Welwood
Learning Experience
Calgary, Alberta, CA

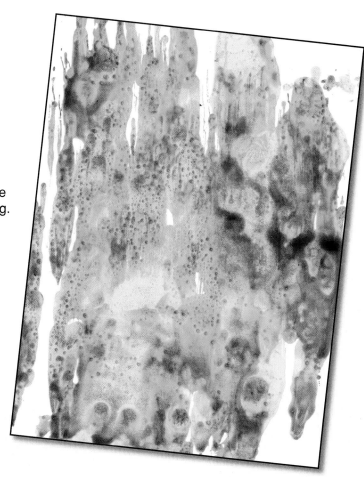

Pleasing Penguins

To make this adorable project, use a chubby paintbrush to dab black paint over a large pinecone. Sprinkle iridescent glitter over the wet paint. Then stretch a cotton ball and glue it to the pinecone as shown to make the penguin's belly. When the paint is dry, use craft glue to attach craft foam details. If desired, display the penguin in a foam tray with packing peanut ice. This chilly little friend is oh so cute!

Karla West
Florence Bowser Elementary
Suffolk, VA

Arts & Crafts for Little Hands

"Purr-fect" Valentine Boxes

This unique cardholder is the cat's meow! To make one, cut off and discard the top half of a cereal box. Cover the remaining half with construction paper. Turn a large heart cutout upside down and add small heart cutouts (ears) and other details to the large heart to make a cat's head. To complete the project, glue the head, a personalized heart, a tail cutout, and two paw cutouts to the box as shown. What a creative way to recycle!

Nancy Garris
Winslow Elementary
Winslow, IN

Presidential Print

To make this Abraham Lincoln likeness, paint a youngster's fingers black and her palm beige. Have her press her hand onto a sheet of white construction paper. Then use a paintbrush to fill in any gaps in the print. When the paint is dry, have her use a marker to add facial details to the print. Finally, trim around the print; then help her cut out and glue a paper top hat to the cutout.

Bobbi Kolacki
Bright Beginnings Preschool
Loganville, GA

Pot of Gold

There really is a pot of gold at the end of this rainbow! Flatten gold mini cupcake liners and then glue them to the top edge of a black pot cutout. Next, glue lengths of different-colored crepe paper along the bottom edge of the pot so they resemble a rainbow. Personalize the project with a gold glitter pen.

Janet Boyce
Cokato, MN

It's a Volcano!

To make this fun craft, trim a paper plate as shown. Then bend and staple the plate to make a volcano shape. Brush thinned white glue over the volcano and press brown tissue paper squares over the wet glue. If needed, brush the volcano with additional layers of glue. When the volcano is dry, twist pieces of red and orange tissue paper and push them into the opening to resemble erupting lava. If desired, attach dinosaur cards (see page 291) to sections of cardboard tube to make them self-standing; then arrange the dinosaurs around the volcano.

Janet Boyce

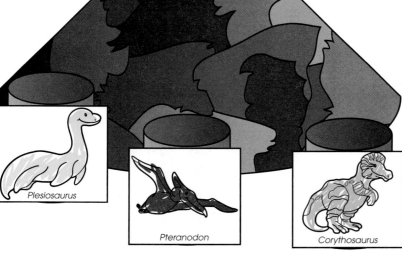

Plesiosaurus

Pteranodon

Corythosaurus

Triceratops

Arts & Crafts for Little Hands

Chocolate Bunny

To make this adorable bunny, cut out a white construction paper copy of the pattern on page 17. Stir a box of chocolate pudding mix into equal amounts of brown paint and glue. Paint the bunny with a thick layer of the mixture; then place candy sprinkles on the mixture. When the project is dry, decorate it with a satin ribbon as shown. These bunnies smell yummy enough to eat!

Melissa Jimenez
Easter Seals Dupage
Villa Park, IL

Wiggly Worms

Rubber worms are the key to this entertaining process art. Obtain several rubber fishing worms. Grasp one end of each worm with a spring-style clothespin; then tape the clothespin closed. Simply drag the loose end of a worm through a shallow container of paint and then wiggle or drag the worm across a sheet of paper. Apply more paint as needed.

Brandi Fields
St. Luke's Hospital Child Care Center
Kansas City, MO

Handmade Chili Pepper

To make a pepper, paint the top of your hand green and the palm and fingers of your hand red. Press your hand onto a sheet of orange construction paper, keeping your fingers close together. When the paint is dry, cut around the handprint so it resembles a pepper shape. Then decorate the pepper with a paper sombrero, a mustache, and sunglasses. That's one red-hot chili pepper!

Bobbi Kolacki
Bright Beginnings Preschool
Loganville, GA

Sweet Strawberry Basket

Dissolve one package of unsweetened strawberry drink mix in four tablespoons of water. To make a basket, use green-tinted water to paint the top edge of a funnel-shaped coffee filter; then paint the remaining portion of the filter using the strawberry water. After the filter is dry, use a round-end toothpick to dab on red paint (strawberry seeds). Attach a green construction paper handle as shown.

Janet Boyce
Cokato, MN

Arts & Crafts for Little Hands

A "Bear-y" Special Message

Here's a card that's just perfect for someone special on Father's Day! To make one, cut out a large brown construction paper bear like the one shown. Glue construction paper shapes to the bear to make paws, ears, and a face; then draw details as desired. Next, cut out a copy of the poem on page 18 and glue it to the bear. When the glue is dry, sign the card and fold the bear's arms to conceal the poem. The lucky recipient is sure to feel loved when he opens this adorable card!

Diane White
Burlington Parks and Recreation Department Preschool
Burlington, Ontario, Canada

You Are "Bear-y" Special!

Roses are red.
Violets are blue.
This little bear
Has a big hug for you!

Picnic Windsock

To make this windsock, cut picnic-related food items from grocery store circulars and glue them to a paper plate. Next, make red or black fingerprints on the plate so they resemble ants. Use a permanent marker to add details to each ant. Finally, glue red and white crepe paper strips to the bottom edge of the plate and attach a string for hanging. How cute!

Karen Eiben
The Learning House Preschool
La Salle, IL

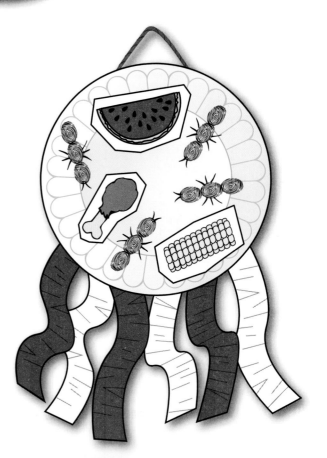

Bunny Pattern
Use with "Before You Read" on page 152 and
"Chocolate Bunny" on page 14.

TEC41042

Heart Poem Pattern

Use with "A 'Bear-y' Special Message" on page 16.

You Are "Bear-y" Special!

Roses are red.
Violets are blue.
This little bear
Has a big hug for you!

TEC41043

You Are "Bear-y" Special!

Roses are red.
Violets are blue.
This little bear
Has a big hug for you!

TEC41043

Busy Hands

Busy Hands

Seasonal Explorations for Little Hands

ideas contributed by Tricia Brown, Bowling Green, KY

WHEELS ON THE BUS

Place an oversize poster board school bus drawing at a table along with glue and wagon wheel pasta tinted yellow. Each youngster visits the center and glues yellow pasta wheels to the school bus.

SNAP AND SORT

Glue circle cutouts of different colors inside the sections of a muffin tin. Place a container of unwrapped crayon stubs in corresponding colors next to the tin. A child snaps the crayons into pieces and then sorts the pieces into the matching color sections. If desired, remove the paper circles and melt the broken crayons in an oven to create chunky crayons.

RED LIKE AN APPLE

Place large red, green, and yellow apple cutouts at a center. Also provide a container of craft items in matching colors. A youngster chooses a craft item and then glues it to the matching apple. Students continue to visit the center until all the items have been glued to the apples.

PASTA PORTRAITS

Dye several different types of pasta and place them at a table along with glue and head outlines as shown. A youngster glues pasta to the outline to make hair and features that resemble his own.

Laura Canavan, The Chestnut Children's Center
Needham, MA

APPLE PICKUP

An apple tree has dropped apples all around the room! Place apple cutouts in your classroom and provide a bushel basket. A youngster takes the basket around the room, collecting apple cutouts as she goes.

Busy Hands

Seasonal Explorations for Little Hands

Pumpkins, spiderwebs, candy corn, and more—you're sure to rake in the compliments on these engaging fine-motor activities!

ideas contributed by Tricia Brown, Bowling Green, KY

PUMPKIN POUNDING

Place a large pumpkin on a table along with a toy hammer, a pair of pliers, and a container of plastic golf tees. A child hammers golf tees into the pumpkin; then she removes each golf tee using the pliers. What a fun way to strengthen muscles and coordination!

Barb Seeton, Prairie College Elementary, Canton, OH

COLORFUL CANDY CORN

Cut apart colorful candy corn cutouts. A youngster arranges the pieces to make candy corn in a variety of different colors.

SUPERSIZE WEB!

Attach a large web cutout to a tabletop. A youngster drags lengths of black yarn through diluted glue and then places the lengths on the cutout. After each child has had the opportunity to add to the web, glue plastic spiders to the project and then display it in the classroom.

PRETTY PUTTY

Put equal amounts of glue and liquid starch in a container; then add a few drops of yellow and red food coloring. Knead the mixture until it reaches the consistency of putty. A youngster cuts, manipulates, and plays with the putty with a variety of tools and seasonal toys. (When not in use, refrigerate the putty in an airtight container.)

PUMPKIN CREATIONS

Little ones have fun creating their own jack-o'-lantern characters! Provide several pumpkin cutouts of different sizes along with a variety of craft foam shapes. A child arranges the pumpkins as desired; then she places shapes on the cutouts to complete her character.

Busy Hands

Seasonal Explorations for Little Hands

Candy canes, snowflakes, snowmen, and more! These ideas are a fun way for little hands to explore popular holiday-themed items.

ideas contributed by Tricia Kylene Brown, Bowling Green, KY

CANDY CANE CREATION

Place an oversize poster board candy cane drawing with stripe outlines at a table along with glue and red-tinted wagon wheel pasta. Each child visits the center and glues on pasta wheels to fill in the candy cane stripes.

INDOOR SNOWFALL

Snowflakes have fallen inside the classroom! Place cotton balls around the room. Provide a pair of mittens and a plastic pail and shovel. A youngster dons the mittens and walks around the room shoveling the mock snowflakes and putting them in the pail.

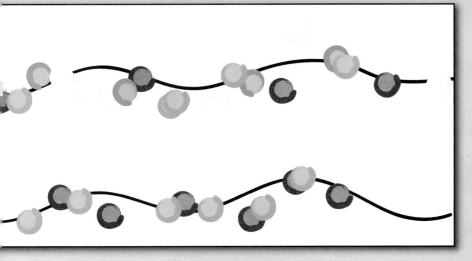

BEAUTIFUL LIGHTS!

Draw wavy lines on a length of butcher paper as shown; then mount the paper on a wall. Provide lidded film canisters and shallow containers of paint. Each child dips the lidded end of a film canister in paint and then presses it onto the paper below a line. The process is repeated until each line resembles a string of lights.

CHUBBY SNOWMAN

Place a large poster board snowman at a table with a supply of cotton balls and glue. Each youngster visits the center and glues cotton balls inside the outline. After the outline is filled in, have students add collage materials, such as large buttons, fabric scraps, twigs, and craft foam–carrot noses.

HOLIDAY GREETINGS

Place a collection of greeting cards and envelopes along with several markers and a class list of names near a holiday-themed mailbox. Youngsters decorate, sign, and then "mail" their cards as well as check for incoming greetings!

Fine-Motor Explorations for the Season

COOKIE DOUGH

Place a batch of scented play dough (recipe below) at a table along with rolling pins, heart-shaped cookie cutters, and cookie sheets. A child flattens a lump of dough with a rolling pin; then she uses the cookie cutters to make heart-shaped cookies. She puts the cookies on a sheet and pretends to bake them. What a scrumptious smell!

adapted from an idea by Tonya Jensen, Heartland Child Development Council Bluffs, IA

Scented play dough recipe: Mix together 4 cups of sifted flour, 1 cup of salt, and 4 packages of unsweetened cherry Kool-Aid drink mix. Add 6 table-spoons of vegetable oil, 4 cups of boiling water, and food coloring. Mix well and then knead the dough when it's cool enough to handle. Store the play dough in an airtight container.

LEPRECHAUN BRACELETS

Provide a supply of green tagboard bracelets (or empty masking tape rings) and holiday-related stickers. A youngster peels a sticker from the backing and presses it onto a bracelet. He continues decorating his bracelet until he is satisfied with his work.

adapted from an idea by Suzanne Foote
East Ithaca Preschool
Ithaca, NY

DR. SEUSS'S EGG

Youngsters fingerpaint a supersize fried egg cutout with light green paint. Then they help drizzle green-tinted corn syrup on the project to make a yolk. Allow several days for the project to dry and then display it in the classroom.

adapted from an idea by Peg Kennedy
Alpha School
Lakewood, NJ

PRIDE OF LIONS

Place yellow cupcake liners at a center along with scissors and a black marker. A child fringe-cuts the edges of several cupcake liners so they resemble lion manes. She draws a face on each lion and then glues her lions to a length of green bulletin board paper. Her classmates repeat the process until there's a huge pride of lions on the paper.

Betsy Butler, Jefferson Brethren Preschool, Goshen, IN

SHAMROCK SURPRISE!

Tape a variety of die-cut shapes and a few shamrock cutouts to a tabletop; then attach a length of bulletin board paper over the cutouts. A child rubs the side of an unwrapped crayon over the surface of the paper, revealing the hidden shapes. When he reveals a shamrock shape he says, "Shamrock surprise!" Replace the paper, as needed.

Penny Waddingham
Grimes, IA

Busy Hands

Fine-Motor Explorations for the Season

ideas contributed by Tricia Brown, Bowling Green, KY

FROG FUN

Place craft foam lily pads in your water table. Provide a plastic frog and a squirt bottle filled with water. A child places the frog on a lily pad and then uses the bottle to squirt the lily pad so it moves across the water's surface.

BEAUTIFUL BUTTERFLIES

Provide an assortment of colorful fabric squares along with plastic spring-style clothespins. A youngster gathers a fabric square and then grasps the center of the gathered material with a clothespin. He gently "flies" the resulting butterfly around the room.

SELF-STICK FLOWERS

Draw several leaves and stems on a length of bulletin board paper. Then place the paper at a table along with self-adhesive craft foam shapes. Youngsters peel the backing from the shapes and press them above the stems to make flowers.

SOFT AS A BUNNY

Place both soft and hard items in a tub and then place the tub at a center along with a bunny cutout. (If desired, use the bunny pattern on page 17.) Encourage youngsters to explore the textures of the items and then place only soft items on the bunny.

KITE CLIPS

Mount on a wall or table a large kite cutout with a tail made of jumbo paper clips. Attach a magnet to each of several different-colored bow cutouts and place them near the kite. A youngster chooses a bow, names the color, and then attaches it to the kite tail. She continues adding bows as desired.

Busy Hands

Fine-Motor Explorations for the Season

ideas contributed by Janet Boyce, Cokato, MN

FESTIVE FLAG

Place a large poster board flag drawing at a table along with glue and a supply of red, white, and blue tissue paper squares. Glue an appropriately colored square to each section of the flag as a color guide. Youngsters visit the center and glue matching squares to the flag. After each child has had the opportunity to decorate the flag, add adhesive stars to the project and then display it in the classroom.

SANDPAPER CASTLES

Place a length of light brown bulletin board paper (beach) on your floor along with a plastic pail filled with sandpaper shapes. A child arranges the shapes on the beach to create her own unique sand castle.

GIANT GOLF BALL

Mount an oversize white circle above a golf tee cutout on a wall. Provide a shallow container of light gray paint and several golf tees. Each child dips the round end of a golf tee in the paint and then presses it on the circle. Youngsters repeat the process until the circle resembles the dimpled surface of a golf ball.

PICNIC ANTS

Cover a table with a plastic picnic-style tablecloth and plastic food. Provide play dough and a supply of small pipe cleaner pieces. A youngster uses the play dough and pipe cleaners to make ants to add to the picnic!

Play Dough

CUTTING THE GRASS

Fill a plastic tub with green paper strips. Provide regular and decorative-edged safety scissors. Little ones visit the center and use the scissors to cut the grass. Later, they use the grass cuttings to add to summer-themed artwork.

Go to page 32 for a reproducible fine-motor activity!

Fr—t—n-we—n—

Note to the teacher: Have students crumple tissue paper squares and glue them to the page to fill in the top of the snow cone.

CIRCLE TIME

Circle Time

Kids Come Marching!

Gather little ones for circle time using this fun song. Lead youngsters in singing the first verse of the song shown as they march to your circle-time area. Then have youngsters sit on the floor as you lead them in singing the remaining verse.

(sung to the tune of "When the Saints Go Marching In")

Oh, when the kids come marching in;
Oh, when the kids come marching in.
Oh, I want to be in that circle
When the kids come marching in.

Oh, when the kids have sat right down;
Oh, when the kids have sat right down.
We will have some fun in our circle
When the kids have sat right down.

Karen Amatrudo, Circle Nursery School, Madison, CT

Special Star

Youngsters develop color-recognition skills with this cute idea! Spread colorful star cutouts on the floor in the center of your circle-time area. Recite the rhyme shown and then invite a volunteer to find a corresponding star and hold it in the air. After confirming that the color is correct, have her place the star back on the floor. Continue in the same manner with each remaining color.

Twinkle, twinkle, [purple] star.
Who can show me where you are?

Rachel Blevins, Children's Center, Middletown, OH

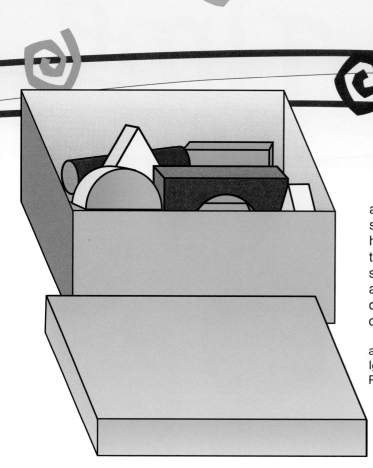

Mystery Sounds

Youngsters will become familiar with classroom objects and how to use them properly with this activity! Conceal several blocks inside a lidded box. Shake the box and have students try to identify the contents from the sound; then open the box to reveal the blocks. Next, bring youngsters to the block center and discuss how to use the blocks appropriately. Repeat the activity with boxes filled with other classroom items, such as paintbrushes from the art center and plastic food from the housekeeping area.

adapted from an idea by Susanna Chin
Ignacio Cruz Early Childhood Learning Center
Perth Amboy, NJ

Wiggly Worms

For each child, cut a hole in a small paper plate. Have each child decorate her plate so it resembles an apple. Then invite each child to hold her apple in one hand and pretend her pointer finger on her other hand is a worm as you lead the group in reciting the fingerplay shown.

Here's a wiggly little worm	*Wiggle pointer finger (worm).*
Looking for some lunch.	*Move worm as if looking around.*
He sees a shiny apple	*Point worm at apple.*
That looks good enough to munch.	
He opens up his mouth	
And takes a bite so wide,	*Have worm "bite" the apple.*
He pops right through the apple	*Poke worm through hole in apple.*
And comes out the other side!	*Wiggle worm.*

adapted from an idea by Kim Montanye
Glyndon United Methodist Preschool
Glyndon, MD

Circle Time

Who Took the Pumpkin?

Place several pumpkin cutouts on the floor. As students cover their eyes, tap a child and have him quietly take a pumpkin and hide from his classmates' view. Next, instruct the remaining youngsters to open their eyes. Lead the group in chanting, "Who took the pumpkin from the pumpkin patch?" Invite volunteers to guess which classmate took the pumpkin. After the child's name has been revealed, have him return to the circle and place the cutout back in the patch.

Jackie Sachs, Jackie's Daycare, Montevideo, MN

A cat comes next!

Living and Nonliving

For this patterning activity, cut out several copies of the cat and ball cards on page 47. Hold up a cat and a ball cutout and have students identify the pictures and then discuss which object pictured is alive and which is not. Next, give each child either a cat or a ball card. Begin a pattern on the floor with extra cutouts. Then have youngsters place their cutouts on the floor to continue the pattern. Help them read aloud the pattern. Then repeat the activity with the remaining cards on page 47.

Kelly Tincher, Head Start, Fort Dodge, IA

Go to page 122 for further exploration of the concept of living and nonliving!

Hurry, Scurry!

Students practice counting with this fun game of hide-and-seek! Place a class supply of acorn cutouts around the room. Tell youngsters they are going to pretend to be hungry little squirrels; then read aloud the rhyme shown. After you say, "Go, go, go," encourage each of your little squirrels to find one acorn and bring it back to his seat. Then lead the class in counting aloud the total number of acorns that were found.

Squirrels, squirrels, bushy and gray,
Please find the acorns right away!
Winter is coming and it will snow.
Find the acorns—go, go, go!

Sue Fleischmann
Sussex, WI

Apples and Pumpkins

To prepare for this activity, make a Venn diagram and title the sections as shown. Also obtain an apple and a pumpkin. To begin, pass each item around the circle for students to examine. Encourage youngsters to describe each item's color, shape, size, weight, smell, and texture; then record student responses in the appropriate sections of the diagram. Next, cut each item in half and repeat the process. Finally, use the information written on the diagram to review with students the similarities and differences between apples and pumpkins.

Tina Borek
Gate Way Christian
Albuquerque, NM

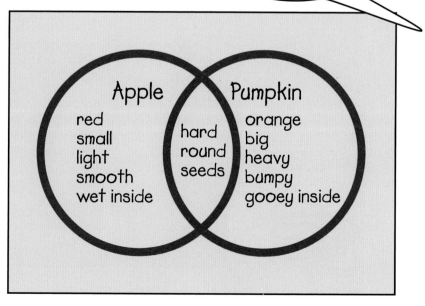

Circle Time

Here I am.

Sleepy Bears

Give each child a colorful bear cutout (see page 48). Then have youngsters curl up on the floor pretending to be bears asleep in a cave. Next, sing the first two lines of the song shown. Have students with the appropriate bears wake up and hold their bears in the air as they sing the third and fourth lines. Then finish singing the song as students pretend to go back to sleep. Repeat the song several times, substituting the remaining color names.

(sung to the tune of "Where Is Thumbkin?")

Where is [red] bear?
Where is [red] bear?
Here I am.
Here I am.
Time to go to sleep now.
Time to go to sleep now.
Until spring.
Until spring.

Lori Connors
Schuylkill I.U. #29
Marlin, PA

Sarah	10
Jon	8
Morgan	22
Lee	10
Jana	18

Edible Coins

Youngsters estimate and count with this idea! Place chocolate Hanukkah gelt in a plastic jar. Pass the jar around the circle and have each child guess the number of coins it contains; write each child's name and guess on a sheet of chart paper. Lead the class in counting the coins aloud as you remove them from the jar. After youngsters evaluate their estimates, give each student a coin to unwrap and eat!

Ellen Farina, Hebrew Academy
Margate, FL

38

Ready, Set, Throw!

Little ones get a gross-motor workout with this fun activity! Divide the class in half and have the groups face each other. Give each child a large white pom-pom (snowball). Play a recording of lively music and have students throw the snowballs at one another. Stop the music and have youngsters stand as still as snowmen. Continue play for several rounds.

Shelley Hoster
Jack & Jill Early Learning Center
Norcross, GA

Student Snowpal

Put a small white sheet or blanket on the floor. Have a volunteer (snowpal) roll on the blanket, wrapping himself with it as you lead the remaining youngsters in singing the first verse of the song shown. At the end of the verse, help him stand; then invite volunteers to dress the snowpal in a hat and scarf as you lead the class in singing the next two verses. During the final verse, have the students wiggle their fingers in the air to resemble sun rays and have the snowpal slowly melt to the floor.

(*sung to the tune of "London Bridge"*)

Roll the snowballs big and round,
Big and round, big and round.
Roll the snowballs big and round.
Build a snowpal!

Put a hat upon his head,
On his head, on his head.
Put a hat upon his head.
Dress the snowpal!

Additional verses:
Wrap a scarf around his neck. Dress the snowpal!
In the sun he'll slowly melt. Goodbye, snowpal!

adapted from an idea by Jackie Sachs
Jackie's Daycare
Montevideo, MN

Circle Time

Heart Hunt

Students practice following directions with this nifty idea! In advance, program a class supply of die-cut hearts with different directions, such as "hop three times," "slither like a snake," or "count to ten." Place the hearts around the room. Recite the rhyme shown. Then encourage each child to find one heart and bring it back to his seat. Read aloud a child's heart and then prompt all the students to follow the directions. Repeat the process for each heart.

Hearts are all around the room.
Find one now—zoom, zoom, zoom!

Hop three times.

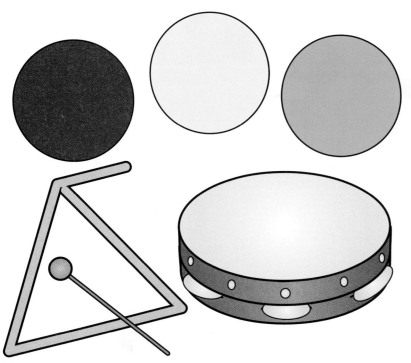

Musical Stop 'n' Go

Provide each child with an instrument; then hold up a green circle cutout and encourage students to play their instruments quickly. Hold up a yellow circle and prompt them to play slowly, and hold up a red circle and encourage them to stop playing. Once students have had the chance to practice these visual commands, try switching your directional signs quickly for some added fun and giggles!

Karla Broad
Our Savior Preschool
Naples, FL

Where's the Leprechaun?

Youngsters pretend to be detectives as they follow a leprechaun's clues! Hide a St. Patrick's Day–related hat in the room. Program paper shamrocks with clues that lead from one area of the room to another and then to the hidden hat. Place each shamrock in the appropriate area. Tell youngsters a leprechaun is hiding in the room and left clues to help the class find him. Then lead your little detectives on a leprechaun search, reading the clues aloud as you go. When you reach the hat, reveal it with great dismay. Then conclude the activity by asking each child what they think happened to that tricky little leprechaun!

adapted from an idea by Karen Valentine
BHK Child Development
South Range, MI

Go to the shelf where we keep our big books.

Go to the area where we play dress-up.

Go to the spot where we play with blocks. I'll be waiting!

Delivering Letters

Put a different letter card in each of several envelopes; then place the envelopes in a tote bag. Give the bag to a volunteer and ask her to pretend she is a mail carrier. Next, play a recording of music and have the mail carrier walk around the outside of the circle. When you stop the music, instruct her to hand an envelope to a classmate. Have the recipient remove the card from the envelope and hold it in the air; then have the class identify the letter. Finally, have the two students switch places. Repeat the process until all the mail has been delivered.

Circle Time

ROAR!

Lion or Baby

Arrange a class supply of chairs in a circle and place an *L* or *B* card under each chair. Have students walk around the chairs as you play a recording of music. When you stop the music, direct each child to take a seat and pick up her card. Instruct each child with a letter *L* to hold it in the air and identify its sound. Then say, "*L* is for lion," and encourage each child to roar like a lion. Repeat the process for youngsters with *B*s, saying, "*B* is for baby," prompting each student to cry like a baby. Finally, have each child place her card under her chair and begin again.

Rainy-Day Poem

With this activity, students develop an awareness of words as separate units of print. Make a class supply of the poem on page 49. Have each child attach a raindrop sticker or cutout to a craft stick to make a minipointer. (Be sure to make a copy of the poem and a pointer for yourself!) Display the page and have youngsters watch as you read the poem aloud, pointing to each word with your pointer. Then give each child his paper and pointer. Read each line aloud, encouraging little ones to follow along and point to each word as you read.

adapted from an idea by Louise Frankel
Family Development Day Care, Plainfield, NJ

Spring Rain

Splish, splash,
Drip, drop!
Raindrops fall,
Plip, plop.
Falling faster,
Raindrops race.
Tickle, tickle.
On my face!

adapted from a poem by Nancy C. Allen
Ashley Abbey Learning Center
Mechanicsville, VA

Rainbow Soup

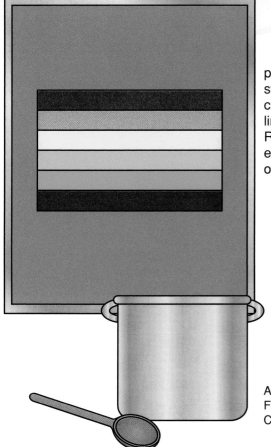

To prepare, cut felt strips in rainbow colors and place them in a soup pot. Then place the pot and a mixing spoon near your flannelboard. Lead students in reciting the first verse of the rhyme shown, encouraging each child to use a stirring motion as you stir the pretend soup. During the final line, remove the red strip from the pot and place it on the flannelboard. Repeat the verse several times, substituting a different color word to match each strip removed from the pot. After placing all the felt strips in rainbow order on the flannelboard, recite the final verse.

What kind of soup is in the pot?
Stir it, stir it, stir it a lot!
Dish some out.
Oh, what could it be?
The prettiest [red] you ever did see!

Final verse:
Rainbow soup was in the pot.
We stirred and stirred it up a lot.
We dished it out, yes sirree!
The prettiest colors you ever did see!

Andrea DelValle and Kristi Welch
Forsyth County Public Library
Cumming, GA

Drip, Drip, Drop

Add a rainy-day twist to the traditional game of Duck, Duck, Goose. Label tagboard raindrops with different numbers. To play, give a child a raindrop. Have him walk around the inside of the circle and say, "Drip," each time he taps a different classmate with his cutout. Instruct him to drop the raindrop in a classmate's lap when he says, "Drop," and then return to his seat. Have the selected child identify the number on the raindrop. Then instruct youngsters to pat their legs the corresponding number of times to imitate the sound of rain.

Mary Robles
Portland, OR

43

Circle Time

Letter Roundup

With this idea, youngsters practice letter identification and get a gross-motor workout! Label horse cutouts (pattern on page 50) with different letters. Then place the horses across the room from your circle-time area. To begin, invite a volunteer to don a cowboy hat. Instruct her to gallop to the horses, choose one, and then gallop back to the circle (corral) with the horse in hand. Have her hold the horse in the air; then have the class identify the letter. Repeat the process until all the horses are in the corral.

Sue Reppert, Widening World Preschool Mentor, OH

Where Is Humpty Dumpty?

Spotlight positional words with help from a familiar nursery rhyme character! Decorate an egg cutout so it resembles Humpty Dumpty and build a small wall using your classroom blocks. To begin, hold the cutout so Humpty Dumpty appears to be sitting on the wall. Then lead students in reciting the traditional rhyme. Next, have a student hold Humpty Dumpty beside the wall. Lead youngsters in reciting the rhyme again, changing the positional word to "Humpty Dumpty sat *beside* a wall." Repeat the process several times, moving Humpty Dumpty in front of, behind, and above the wall.

adapted from an idea by Sue Fleischmann Sussex, WI

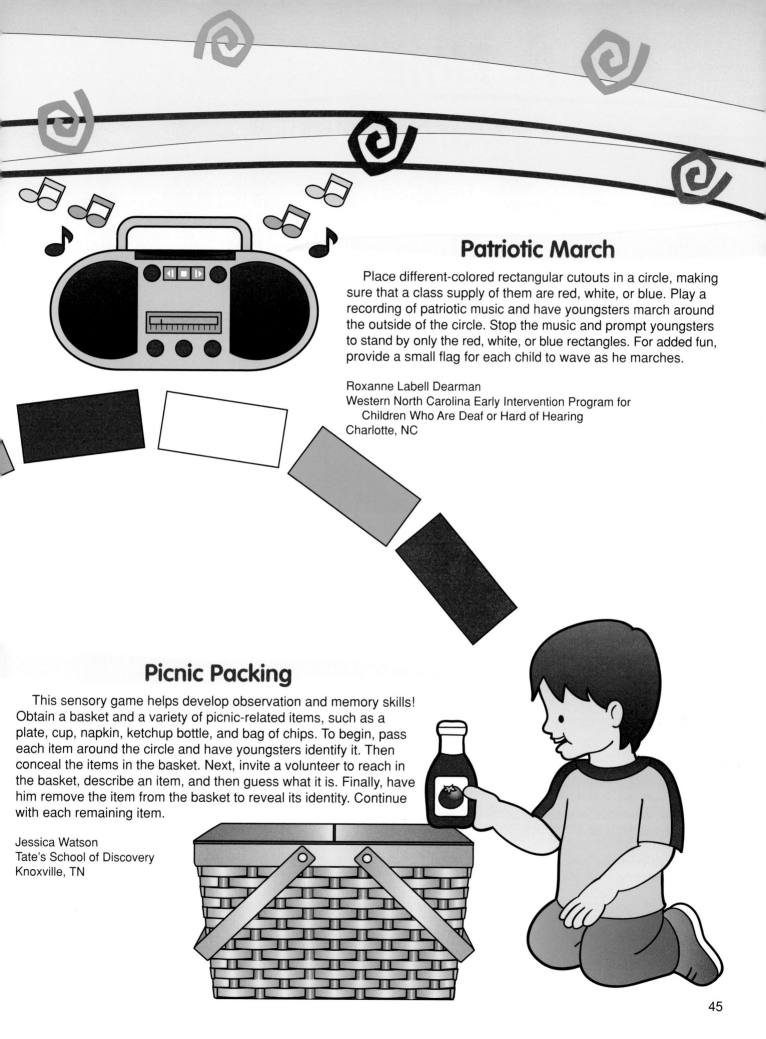

Patriotic March

Place different-colored rectangular cutouts in a circle, making sure that a class supply of them are red, white, or blue. Play a recording of patriotic music and have youngsters march around the outside of the circle. Stop the music and prompt youngsters to stand by only the red, white, or blue rectangles. For added fun, provide a small flag for each child to wave as he marches.

Roxanne Labell Dearman
Western North Carolina Early Intervention Program for
    Children Who Are Deaf or Hard of Hearing
Charlotte, NC

Picnic Packing

This sensory game helps develop observation and memory skills! Obtain a basket and a variety of picnic-related items, such as a plate, cup, napkin, ketchup bottle, and bag of chips. To begin, pass each item around the circle and have youngsters identify it. Then conceal the items in the basket. Next, invite a volunteer to reach in the basket, describe an item, and then guess what it is. Finally, have him remove the item from the basket to reveal its identity. Continue with each remaining item.

Jessica Watson
Tate's School of Discovery
Knoxville, TN

Circle Time

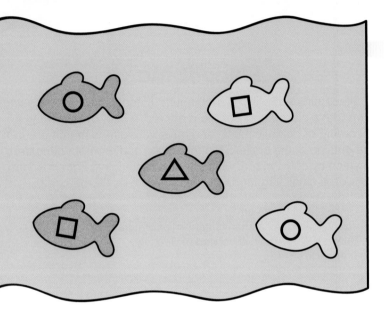

Making Waves

Obtain a blue sheet or shower curtain (ocean). Also label a class supply of fish cutouts with desired shapes. Instruct each child to hold the edge of the ocean; then place the fish in the center. Encourage youngsters to shake the ocean vigorously to create gigantic waves. When all the fish have spilled onto the floor, have each student retrieve a fish. Next, name one of the shapes. Then have each child with a corresponding fish toss it back into the ocean. Continue until all the fish have been returned.

adapted from an idea by Karen Eiben
The Learning House Preschool
La Salle, IL

Beach-Ball Bounce

Invite little ones to pretend they are sitting on the beach. Then have youngsters pass a beach ball around the circle as you lead them in singing the song shown. When the song ends, have the child with the ball call out a classmate's name; then have him bounce the ball to that child. Repeat the process until each child has had a turn to bounce the beach ball to a classmate.

(*sung to the tune of "Ten Little Indians"*)

One little, two little, three little beach balls,
Four little, five little, six little beach balls,
Seven little, eight little, nine little beach balls
Bounce around the shore.

adapted from an idea by Susan Luengen
Makalapa Elementary
Honolulu, HI

Eric

TEC41039

TEC41039

TEC41039

TEC41039

TEC41040

Spring Rain

Splish, splash,

Drip, drop!

Raindrops fall,

Plip, plop.

Falling faster,

Raindrops race.

Tickle, tickle.

On my face!

adapted from a poem by Nancy C. Allen
Ashley Abbey Learning Center
Mechanicsville, VA

Note to the teacher: Use with "Rainy-Day Poem" on page 42.

Horse Pattern
Use with "Letter Roundup" on page 44.

TEC41043

CLASSROOM DISPLAYS

CLASSROOM DISPLAYS

We're a **COLORFUL** Class!

To make this three-dimensional display, have each youngster color a construction paper copy of the crayon pattern from page 64. Encourage her to glue a photo of herself to the crayon as shown. Then help her attach accordion-folded construction paper legs and arms to the crayon. Mount the crayons to a board and title the display "We're a Colorful Class!"

Pam Ballingall, Manchester, NH

We're Bear-y, Bear-y Big!

Have youngsters help sponge-paint an oversize bear cutout. Take a photograph of each child standing next to your growth chart; then record his name and height on the photo. Mount the bear on a wall; then attach the photos to the bear and title the display as shown.

Missy Goldenberg
Beth Shalom Nursery School
Overland Park, KS

Preschool Is More Fun Than a Barrel of Monkeys!

To make this display, encourage each youngster to color and cut out an enlarged copy of the monkey pattern on page 65. Use a permanent black marker to label each monkey with the appropriate child's name. Then mount the monkeys around a barrel cutout on your wall. (Hint: Aluminum foil makes eye-catching hoops for the barrel!) Finally, add the title shown to the display.

Sue Fleischmann
Sussex, WI

Encourage parents to donate items needed for your classroom with the help of this display! Have each child make a flower, similar to the ones shown, by tracing her hand. Then write on each hand the name of an item needed for your classroom. Mount the finished projects on a board along with a copy of the poem shown. Then add the title "Helping Hands."

Starlette Hudson, Play-n-Pretend Preschool, Danville, VA

CLASSROOM DISPLAYS

Midnight Cats

1 big black square
2 medium white squares
3 medium pink squares
2 medium black squares
2 small green squares
6 squiggly white paper strips

I Cute Cat!

Try this cute idea for a "purr-fect" nighttime display! To make a cat, have each child glue together square cutouts as shown; then attach paper strips for whiskers. Mount the projects on a board or wall decorated as shown.

Angie Kutzer, Burlington, NC

Preschool Pizzeria!

To make this yummy-looking display, have each child glue crumpled brown tissue paper to a red triangle cutout so it resembles pizza crust. Encourage him to glue craft item toppings to his pizza slice. Then have him glue white crinkle shreds (cheese) over the toppings. Finally, encourage him to mount the pizza slice on a paper plate. Then display the projects with the title shown.

Tina Auten
Williams Magnet School
Topeka, KS

Let's Talk Turkey!

Have each child make a simple turkey craft as shown. Then ask him what his turkey would say if it could talk. Write his words on a speech bubble cutout. Then attach the turkeys and speech bubbles to a wall in your classroom, along with the title shown.

My feathers are pretty. I like the orange ones best.

"We're 'Gourd-geous'!"

Invite each child to sponge-paint a copy of page 66 using red, brown, green, yellow, and orange paint. After the paint is dry, cut out each gourd. Then have each child glue to her gourd a construction paper stem and a photo of her face. Mount the projects on a board with the title "We're 'Gourd-geous'!"

Pam Ballingall, Gossler Park School, Manchester, NH

CLASSROOM DISPLAYS

We're Ready for Winter!

Have a child glue a craft item to a left-hand mitten cutout; then prompt her partner to glue a matching craft item to a right-hand mitten cutout. The children repeat the process several times, taking turns being first to choose and glue an item. Hole-punch the resulting pairs of mittens and then string them together with a length of yarn. Display the pairs of mittens with the title shown.

Jill Barber, Brookside Elementary, Gastonia, NC

A Kwanzaa Celebration!

For this display, have students make red, green, and black handprints on an oversize basket cutout. Also have youngsters paint fruit cutouts. Attach the basket to a wall and mount the pictures above the basket. Complete the display by attaching corn and unity cup cutouts near either side of the basket; then title the display as shown.

Jill Thurston
Christ Lutheran Day Care
Downey, CA

Puzzles with missing pieces come in handy for this display! Have youngsters glue puzzle pieces to a green poster board tree and then paint the pieces with a mixture of green paint and green glitter. Encourage them to attach circle cutouts to the tree. Then mount the tree on a board and add a star and the title shown.

Twila Grey
Rose Hill United Methodist Youth Center
Rose Hill, KS

To make this three-dimensional display, obtain a class supply of clear plastic fillable ornaments (found at craft stores). Attach a photo cutout of a child to the inside of an ornament; then have the child fill the ornament with garland and sequins. Tie ribbon around the top of each ornament and attach a loop for hanging. Display the ornaments as shown.

Carolyn Winland, Burgett's Child Care Center, West Lafayette, IN

CLASSROOM DISPLAYS

Our Class Is as Good as Gold!

Take headshot photographs of your youngsters using your digital camera. Then enlarge the photos and print them. Cut around each photo. Next, have each child attach his photo to an extra large gold coin cutout. Encourage each child to decorate his project with gold glitter. Then display the coins as shown.

Keely Peasner, Liberty Ridge Head Start, Bonney Lake, WA

This display helps little ones organize data and works well with even the youngest of preschoolers. Post large cutouts related to a current theme in your classroom. Have each student write his name on a sticky note with help as needed. Then encourage him to attach his sticky note to the cutout that represents which object he prefers. If desired, keep this display up all year long, changing the borders and cutouts to match each new theme.

Lisa Bishop
Elizabeth Wilhelm Elementary
North Las Vegas, NV

We're Sweet on Valentine's Day!

Try this idea for a sweet three-dimensional display! Invite each child to glue crumpled brown or white tissue paper to the inside of a foil cupcake liner. Then help her drizzle tinted glue on the tissue paper. When the projects are dry, use double-sided tape to attach them to a large heart cutout so it resembles an oversize box of candy. Mount the heart on a wall and add the title shown.

Amber Knight
Kidd Academy
Grand Prairie, TX

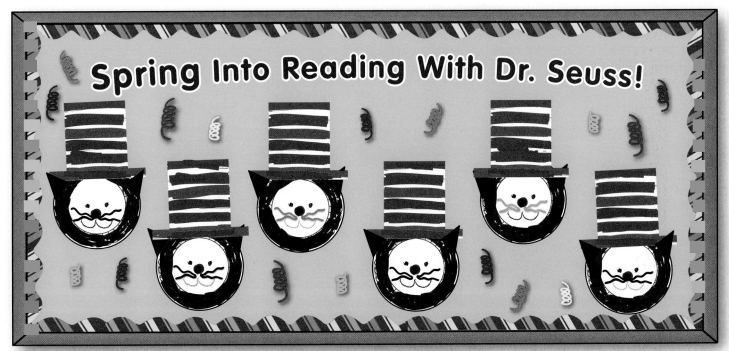

Have each child transform a paper plate into a cat using paint (face), pipe cleaners (whiskers), and construction paper scraps (ears). Then have her paint red stripes on a white hat cutout. When the paint is dry, staple the hat to the plate. Wrap pipe cleaners around pencils and then remove the pipe cleaners to make springs. Attach the projects and the springs to a display with the title shown.

Teresa Montgomery, Hopkins Elementary, Somerset, KY

CLASSROOM DISPLAYS

I'd Pick a Friend Like You!

Have each child color the edge of a coffee filter with washable markers and then spray the filter with water. When the filter is dry, have him transform the filter into a flower by adding a stem and leaves. Then give him a photo of himself to glue to his flower. Encourage each youngster to exchange his flower with a friend. Then mount the flowers on a board decorated and titled as shown.

Christina Hossack, Little Wonders Day School, Jamesburg, NJ

Have an "Egg-cellent" Easter!

To make this display, have each child glue brown crinkle shreds to a paper plate; then have her glue colorful egg cutouts to the crinkle shreds. Next, encourage her to color a white construction paper copy of the chicken pattern from page 63. Then mount the projects on a board decorated to resemble a chicken coop.

Cathy Germino, A Little Folks School House, Manchester, NH

CLASSROOM DISPLAYS

Lifting Off Into Summer!

Welcome summer with this nifty display! To make a hot-air balloon, have each child glue tissue paper squares to a balloon shape. Help him trim any overhanging tissue paper. Then have him make a plastic canvas rubbing on a square piece of paper and attach the resulting basket to the balloon with yarn. Mount the projects on a board decorated as shown.

Kimberly Dessel, Pixie Preschool and Kindergarten, Spotswood, NJ

Lending a Hand to Build a Cozy Campfire!

To make this cozy campfire, have each child sprinkle red, orange, and yellow powdered tempera paint onto a cutout of her hand. Provide a spray bottle filled with water; then encourage her to spray a mist of water onto the cutout to dilute the paint. When the paint is dry, mount the resulting flames above a paper log with the title and details shown.

Jackie Summers
Oneida Nation Elementary
Oneida, WI

Ants in Your Pants!

Provide access to red or black ink pads and markers. Then encourage each child to decorate a copy of page 68 with finger-print ants, as shown, using a fine-tip marker to add details. Then use clothespins to secure the pants to a length of rope attached to a wall. Add the title "Ants in Your Pants!" to complete the display.

Tracy Hahn, The Goddard School, Freehold, NJ

To make this adorable display, enlarge a head shot of each child. Then cut out the enlargements and have each youngster glue her cutout to a paper plate. Instruct her to decorate a hat and bowtie cutout and attach them to her photo. Then encourage her to attach a red pom-pom to the nose on her photo and add any other desired decorations. Mount the projects on a board decorated and titled as shown.

Amber Baker, Learn a Lot Christian Preschool, Moorseville, IN

Preschool Is "Toad-ally" Awesome!

Stir torn, crumpled facial tissue into a mixture of brown and green paint. Encourage each child to dab the paint over a construction paper toad cutout (pattern on page 67). When the project is dry, have him use a cotton swab to dab red paint spots on his toad. Then have him cut eyes and a mouth from paper scraps and glue them in place. Mount the toads on a wall with a rock cutout and fringed paper grass. Then add the title shown.

Kim Dessel
Pixie Preschool and Kindergarten
Spotswood, NJ

Chicken Pattern
Use with "Have an 'Egg-cellent' Easter!" on page 60.

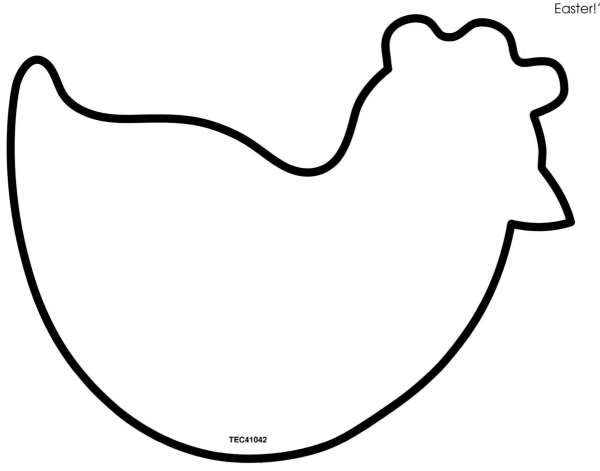

TEC41042

Crayon Pattern
Use with "We're a Colorful Class!" on page 52.

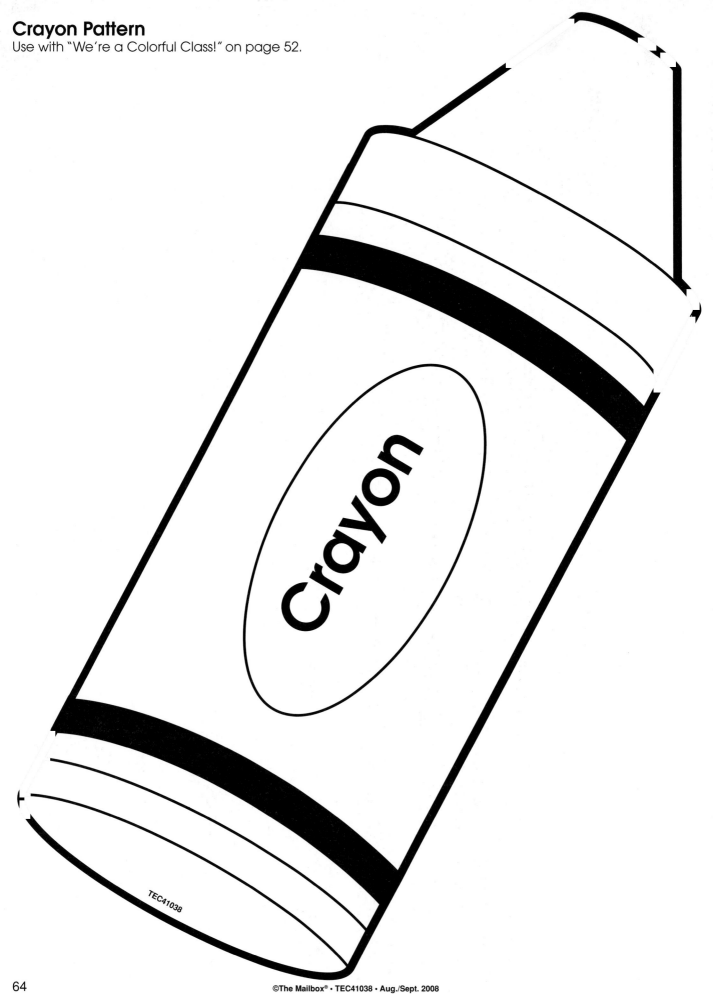

Crayon

TEC41038

Monkey Pattern

Use with "Preschool Is More Fun Than a Barrel of Monkeys!" on page 53, "Monkeys in the Tree" on page 262, and "'A-peeling' Classroom Jobs" on page 264.

TEC41038

Alligator Pattern

Use with "See You Later, Alligator!" on page 263.

TEC41038

Gourd Pattern

Use with "We're 'Gourd-geous'!" on page 55.

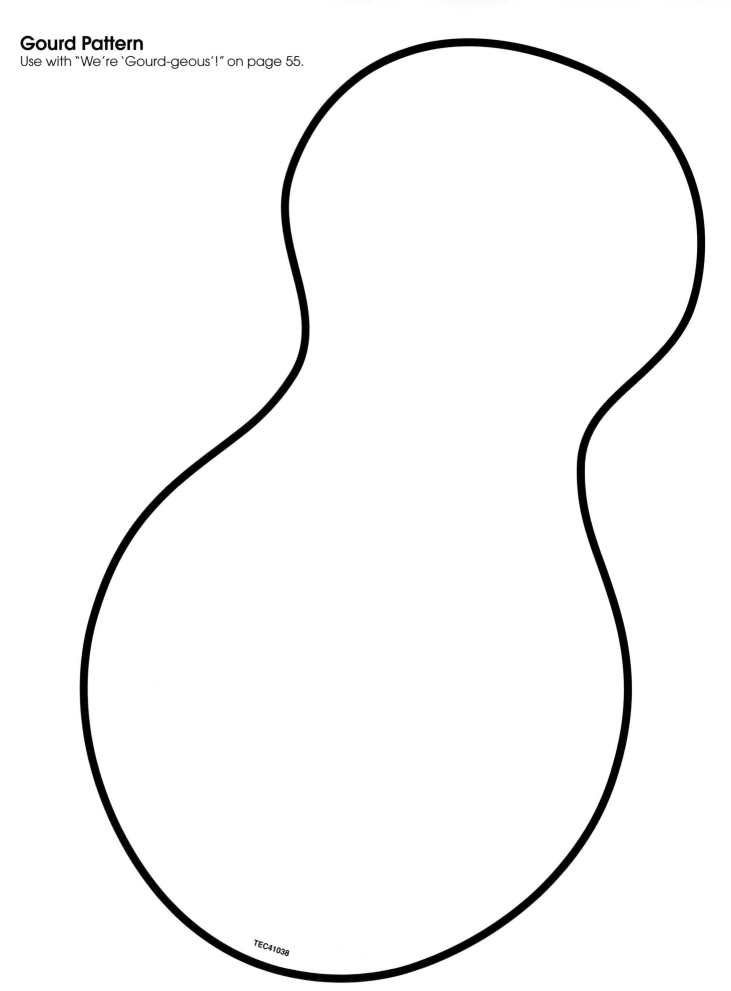

TEC41038

TEC41042

Pants Pattern
Use with "Ants in Your Pants!" on page 62.

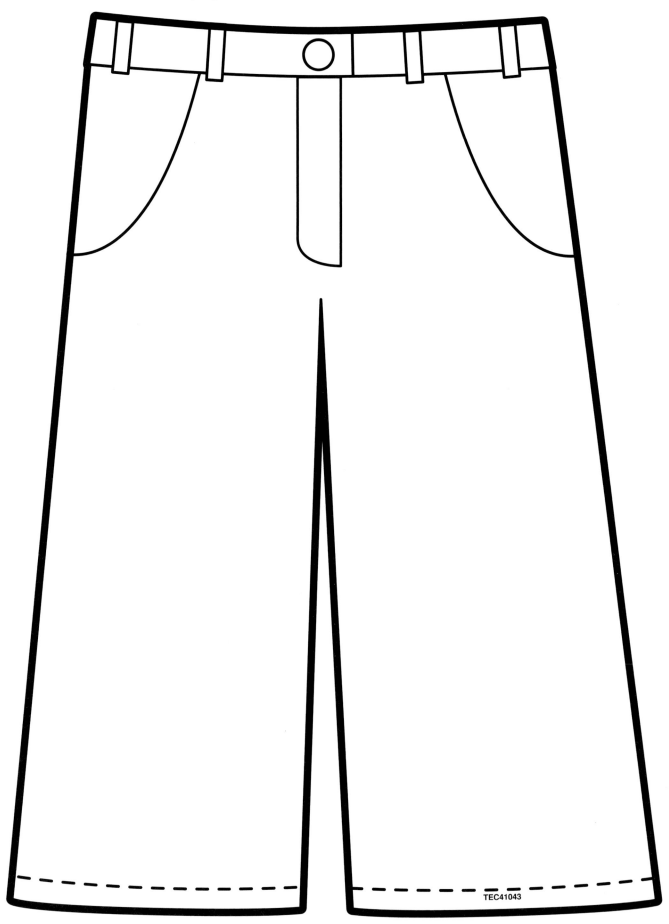

TEC41043

Kids in the Kitchen

Serve up a batch of back-to-school fun with this tasty apple snack.

To prepare for this snack:
- Collect the necessary ingredients and utensils using the lists on the recipe card below.
- Photocopy the step-by-step recipe cards on page 71.
- Color the cards; then cut them out and display them in your snack area.
- Follow the teacher preparation guidelines for the snack.

Apple Burrito

Ingredients for one:
small tortilla, slightly warmed
cinnamon and brown sugar whipped
    cream cheese
thin apple slices

Utensils and supplies:
disposable plate for each child
plastic knife for each child

Teacher preparation:
Arrange the ingredients and supplies near the step-by-step recipe cards.

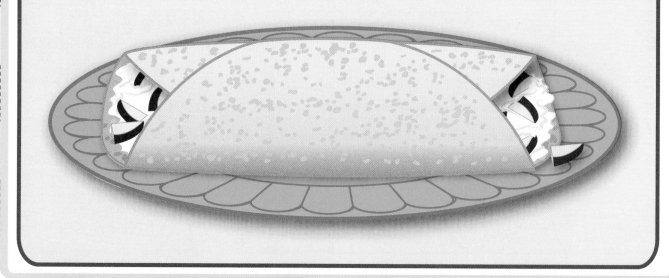

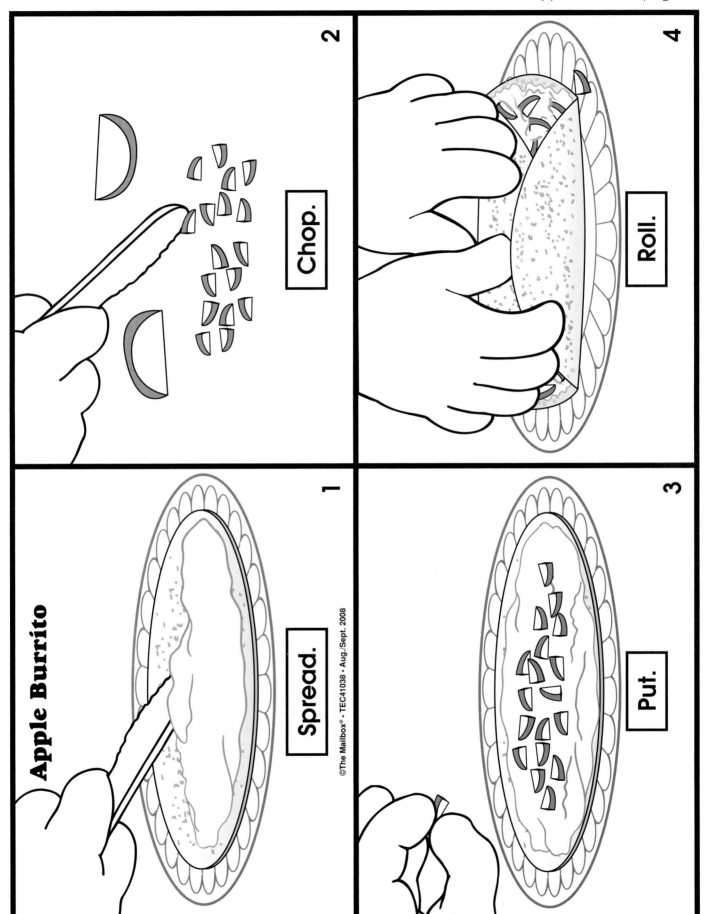

2

Chop.

4

Roll.

Apple Burrito

Spread.

©The Mailbox® · TEC41038 · Aug./Sept. 2008

1

3

Put.

KIDS IN THE KITCHEN

Have youngsters make this tasty turkey snack to add to your Thanksgiving celebration.

To prepare for the snack:
- Collect the necessary ingredients and utensils using the lists on the recipe card below.
- Photocopy the step-by-step recipe cards on page 73.
- Color the cards; then cut them out and display them in the snack area.
- Follow the teacher preparation guidelines for the snack.

Turkey Toppers

Ingredients for one:
⅓ c. cooked turkey or chicken (shredded)
1 tsp. chopped dill pickles
1 tbsp. light mayonnaise
crackers

Utensils and supplies:
bowl for each child
⅓ c. measuring cup
teaspoon
tablespoon
plastic spoon for each child
napkin for each child

Teacher Preparation:
Place the teaspoon and tablespoon in the appropriate ingredients. Arrange the ingredients and supplies near the step-by-step recipe cards.

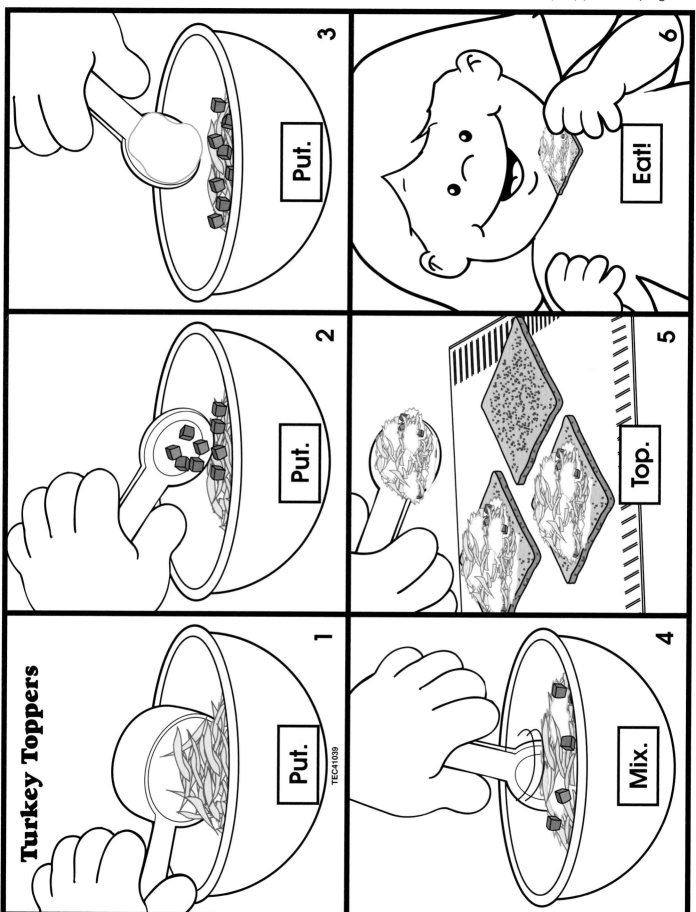

Turkey Toppers

TEC41039

Put.

Put.

Put.

Mix.

Top.

Eat!

KIDS IN THE KITCHEN

Explain to youngsters that bears eat a lot of food before they go to sleep for the winter months. Their meals might include fish, nuts, fruit, and honey. Then invite little ones to make this sleepy-bear snack mix!

To prepare for the snack:
- Collect the necessary ingredients and utensils using the lists on the recipe card below.
- Photocopy the step-by-step recipe cards on page 75.
- Color the cards; then cut them out and display them in the snack area.
- Follow the teacher preparation guidelines for the snack.

Sleepy-Bear Snack Mix

Ingredients for one:
Honeycomb cereal
2 flavors of fish-shaped crackers
shelled sunflower seeds
dried apple slices

Utensils and supplies:
4 large spoons
resealable plastic bag for each child

Teacher preparation:
Arrange the ingredients and supplies near the step-by-step recipe cards.

Jill Butler
Discovery Center for Children
Bellefontaine, OH

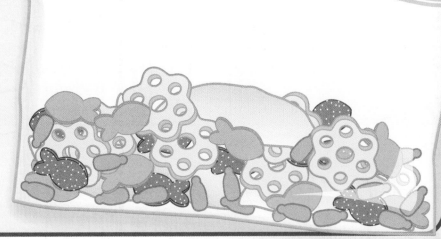

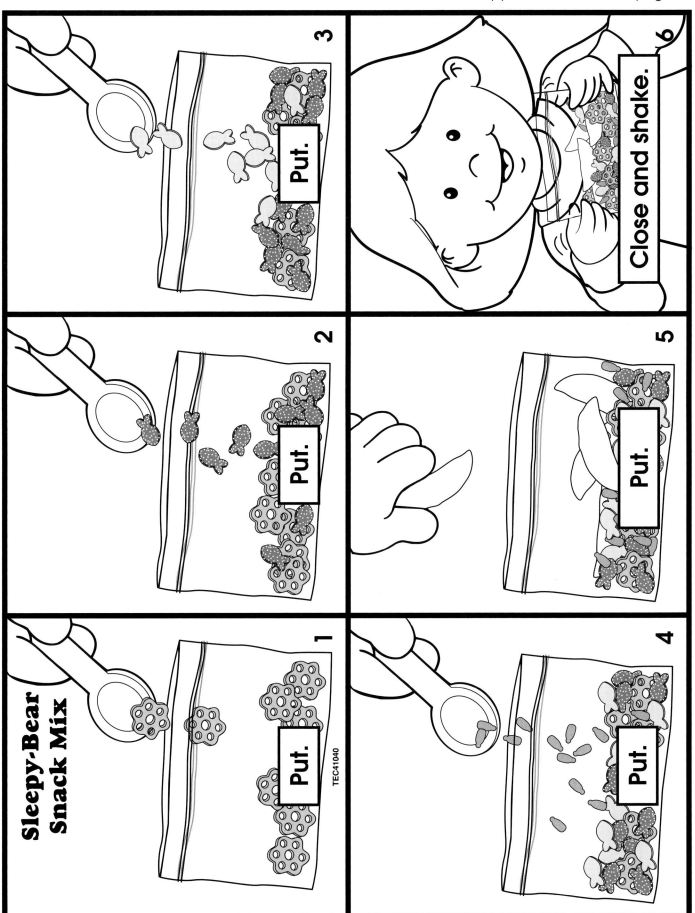

Sleepy-Bear Snack Mix

TEC41040

1 — Put.

2 — Put.

3 — Put.

4 — Put.

5 — Put.

6 — Close and shake.

KIDS IN THE KITCHEN

Show youngsters pictures of several types of butterflies. Encourage them to discuss the variety of wing colors and patterns. Then invite little ones to make their own colorful butterfly snacks.

To prepare for the snack:
- Collect the necessary ingredients and utensils using the lists on the recipe card below.
- Photocopy the step-by-step recipe cards on page 77.
- Color the cards; then cut them out and display them in the snack area.
- Follow the teacher preparation guidelines for the snack.

Colorful Butterfly

Ingredients for one:
graham cracker
tinted frosting
M&M's Minis candies
2 pretzels
colored sprinkles

Utensils and supplies:
disposable plate for each child
plastic knife for each child

Teacher preparation:
Arrange the ingredients and supplies near the step-by-step recipe cards.

Chris Thorson
St. Mary's Lutheran Nursery School
Kenosha, WI

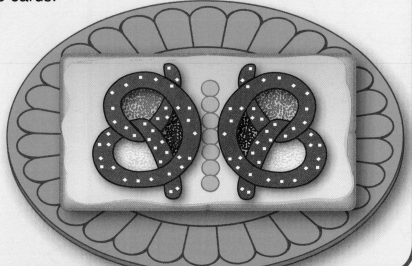

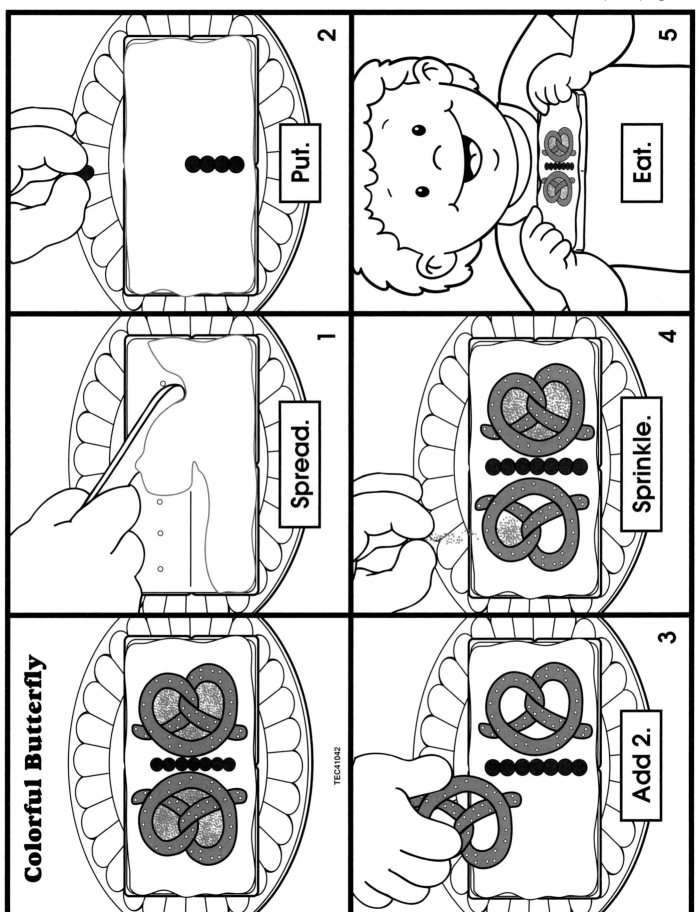

2

Put.

5

Eat.

1

Spread.

4

Sprinkle.

Colorful Butterfly

TEC41042

3

Add 2.

KIDS IN THE KITCHEN

Little ones will delight in arranging bears around their own edible campfires with this snack!

To prepare for the snack:
- Collect the necessary ingredients and utensils using the lists on the recipe card below.
- Photocopy the step-by-step recipe cards on page 79.
- Color the cards; then cut them out and display them in the snack area.
- Follow the teacher preparation guidelines for the snack.

Camping Bears

Ingredients for one:
pretzel sticks
Teddy Grahams graham snacks
orange spray cheese

Utensils and supplies:
disposable plate for each child

Teacher preparation:
Arrange the ingredients and supplies near the step-by-step recipe cards.

Janet Boyce
Cokato, MN

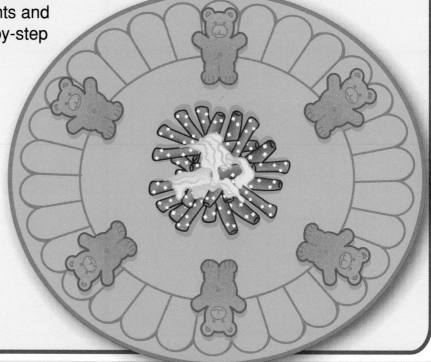

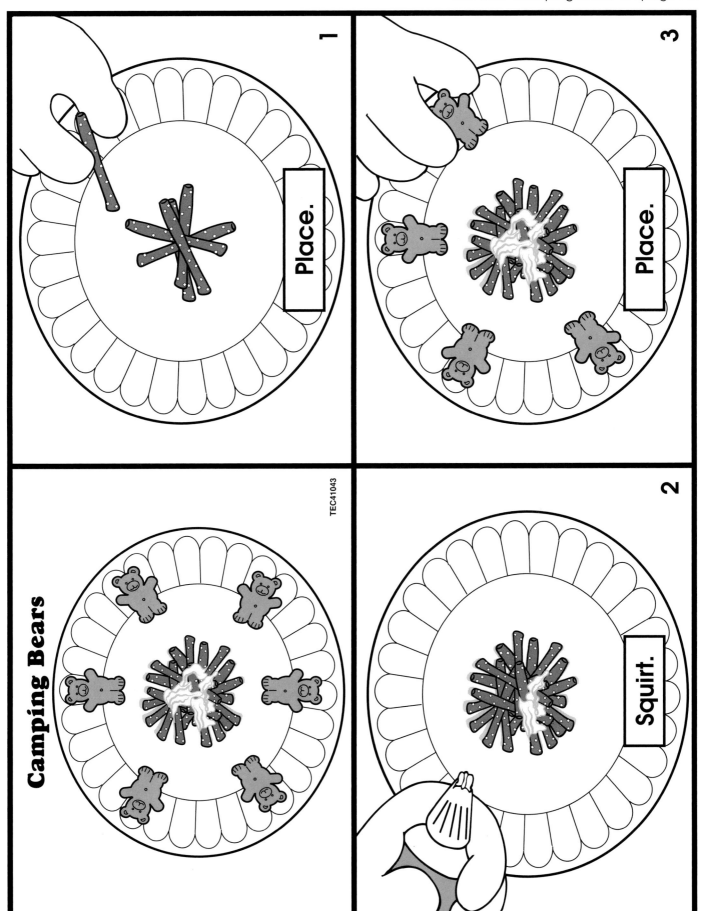

Camping Bears

1

Place.

2

Squirt.

3

Place.

TEC41043

Invite little ones to make and enjoy this delicious dinosaur treat! If desired, incorporate this snack into the dinosaur unit! (See pages 287–291.)

To prepare for the snack:
- Collect the necessary ingredients and utensils using the lists on the recipe card below.
- Photocopy the step-by-step recipe cards on page 81.
- Color the cards; then cut them out and display them in the snack area.
- Follow the teacher preparation guidelines for the snack.

Scrumptious Stegosaurus

Ingredients for one:
banana half (sliced lengthwise)
square cereal pieces
mini chocolate chip

Utensils and supplies:
disposable plate for each child

Teacher Preparation:
Arrange the ingredients and supplies near the step-by-step recipe cards.

Claudia Johnson
Battlefield Park Elementary
Mechanicsville, VA

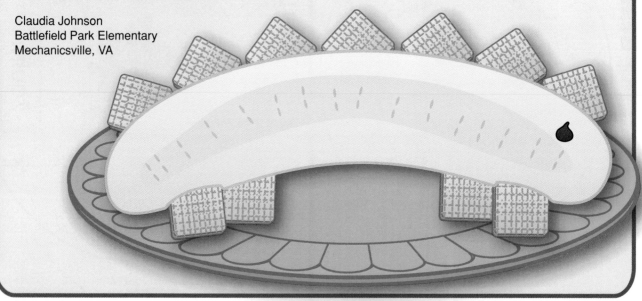

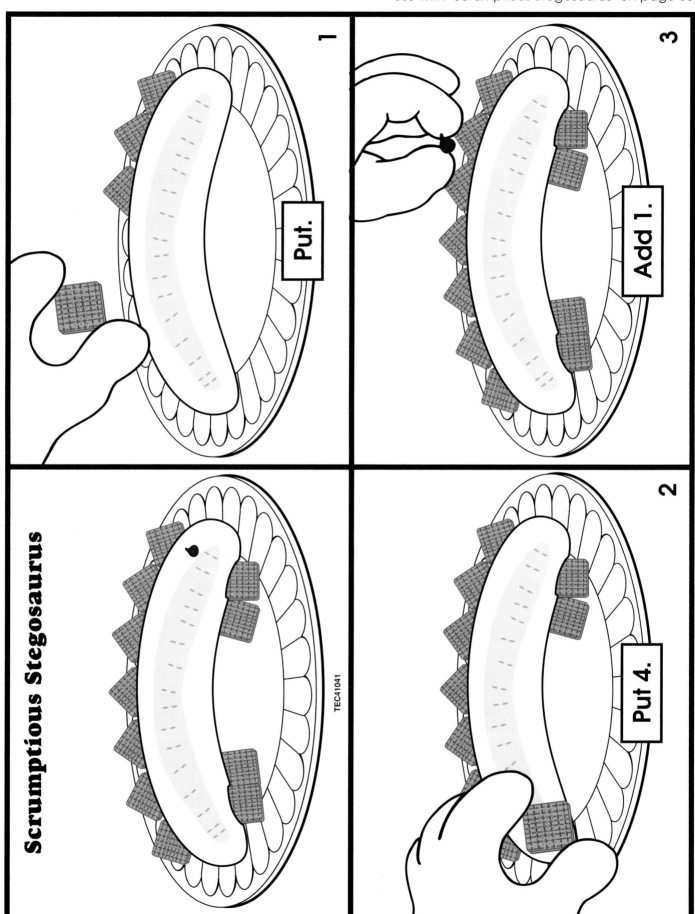

Scrumptious Stegosaurus

1 | Put.

2 | Put 4.

3 | Add 1.

TEC41041

Supply Request Note

Use with "Scrumptious Stegosaurus" on page 80.

Dear Parent/Guardian,
We are making a Scrumptious Stegosaurus soon. We would be grateful if you could help by providing the following ingredient(s):

_____

_____

_____

We need the ingredient(s) listed above by _____.
                                                        date
Please let me know if you are able to send the ingredient(s).

                              Thank you,

                    _____
                              teacher

☐ Yes, I am able to send the ingredient(s).
☐ No, I am unable to send the ingredient(s) this time.

                    _____
                         parent/guardian signature

©The Mailbox® • February/March 2009

Dear Parent/Guardian,
We are making a Scrumptious Stegosaurus soon. We would be grateful if you could help by providing the following ingredient(s):

_____

_____

_____

We need the ingredient(s) listed above by _____.
                                                        date
Please let me know if you are able to send the ingredient(s).

                              Thank you,

                    _____
                              teacher

☐ Yes, I am able to send the ingredient(s).
☐ No, I am unable to send the ingredient(s) this time.

                    _____
                         parent/guardian signature

©The Mailbox® • February/March 2009

LEARNING CENTERS

Learning Centers

CD Clip
Literacy Center

Glue construction paper circles to recycled compact discs; then label each circle with a different letter. Program a supply of spring-style clothespins with letters that correspond to the discs. Place the discs and the clothespins at a center. A child visits the center and clips the clothespins to the matching discs.

Deborah Provencher
West Brookfield Elementary
West Brookfield, MA

Photo Search
Sensory Center

To prepare, print two identical sets of photographs of various classroom materials. Use one set of photographs to label classroom shelves and containers. Place the remaining set of photos in your sensory table along with a supply of shredded paper. A visiting child searches through the shredded paper to find a photograph and then locates the matching photo on a shelf or container in the classroom.

Pamela Butler
Fremont Congregational Nursery School
Fremont, CA

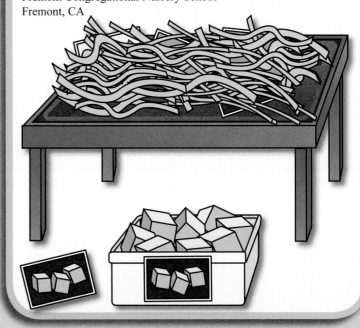

Match Mats
Math Center

Trace the top of a plastic condiment cup on a sheet of construction paper several times. Label each circle with a different shape. Then program the outside bottom of an equal number of condiment cups with corresponding shapes. Place the mat and the condiment cups at a center. A child places each cup over its corresponding shape.

Angela Evans
Crossgates Methodist Children's Center
Brandon, MS

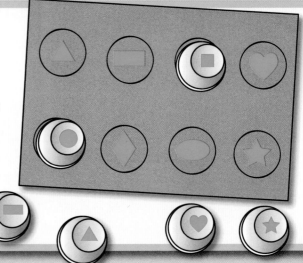

Learning Centers

Beautiful Barrettes
Fine-Motor Area

Draw a face and hair on a small paper plate. Then use a hole puncher to make a hole on each side of the face. Thread several lengths of thick yarn through each hole; then secure the yarn in place. Put the plate at a center along with several large plastic barrettes. A youngster fastens barrettes along the yarn.

Marisol Rodriguez
Holy Innocents Center
Hammond, IN

Seated Self-Portraits
Art Center

Place at a center a class supply of people cutouts. Also provide crayons, collage materials, and an unbreakable mirror. A child looks in the mirror and then decorates a cutout to resemble herself. Then she folds the cutout above the legs and places it in a seated position, as shown.

Janet Boyce
Cokato, MN

Hungry Worms
Play Dough Center

To prepare, cut out several construction paper apple shapes. Laminate each apple to make a nonstick surface. Place the apples at a table along with a supply of green play dough. A child rolls the play dough between his hands to create wormlike shapes. Then he wiggles each worm onto an apple.

Sue Fleischmann
Sussex, WI

Learning Centers

Pumpkin Parts
Sensory Center

Cut a pumpkin into several pieces. Place each piece on a separate tray, leaving the pulp and seeds intact. Place the trays at a center along with several plastic knives and plastic kitchen scrapers. A child describes the smell and textures of the pumpkin; then she uses her fingers or a kitchen tool to remove the pulp and seeds.

Barb Seeton
Prairie College Elementary School
Canton, OH

Spider Toss
Gross-Motor Area

In advance, use an X-ACTO knife to cut several holes in a black tabletop display board (available at office supply stores). Then draw a spiderweb design on the board using a white crayon. Place the display board at a center along with several plastic spiders. A youngster tosses the spiders through the holes in the board.

Ann Smith
Project REACH
Columbia, MO

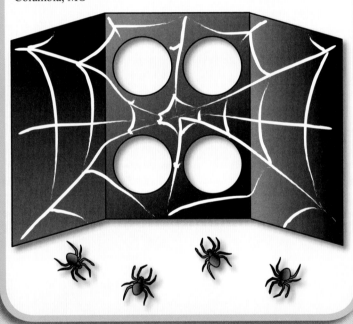

Jack-o'-Lantern Ornaments
Art Center

Obtain a supply of clear plastic ornaments from a local craft store. Place several ornaments at a center along with orange acrylic paint. A student paints the entire surface of an ornament. After the ornament is dry, he adds sponge-printed facial features. Then he attaches a curled green pipe cleaner to the top of the ornament so it resembles a vine.

Bonnie Martin
Hopewell Country Day School
Pennington, NJ

Autumn Leaves
Game Center

Mount a simple poster board tree to a wall. Use temporary adhesive to attach a supply of red, yellow, orange, green, and brown tagboard leaves to the tree. Make a leaf die as shown, designating one side of the die as wild. In turn, each child rolls the die and then removes an appropriate leaf from the tree. If a student rolls the "wild" side, he removes a leaf of his choice. Youngsters continue until all the leaves have "fallen" off the tree.

Elizabeth Cook
Clayton, MO

P Is for Pumpkin!
Literacy Center

To prepare, mix pumpkin spice into a batch of orange play dough. Put the play dough at a center along with rolling pins, small pie tins, and several letter *P* cookie cutters. A child visits the center and uses a rolling pin and play dough to make a pretend pie. She uses a cookie cutter to stamp the letter *P* on top of her pie. Then she identifies the letter name and its sound.

Jennifer Nelson
Lindon Elementary
Lindon, UT

Pizza Patterns
Math Center

Use the patterns on page 94 to make several patterning strips and additional topping cutouts. Make a simple construction paper pizza without toppings. Then place the prepared items at a center. A visiting youngster chooses a pattern and uses the additional toppings to copy the pattern on the pizza.

Roxanne LaBell Dearman
Western NC Early Intervention Program for Children Who Are Deaf or Hard of Hearing, Charlotte, NC

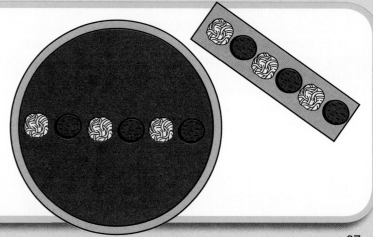

Learning Centers

Bear Caves
Block Center

Put in your block center a supply of silk leaves, small plastic teddy bears, and medium-size rocks. A youngster uses blocks to build caves for the bears to hibernate in. He embellishes the caves with rocks and lines the caves with comfortable leaves. If desired, provide bear-themed picture books for youngsters to use for inspiration in pretend play with the bears and homemade caves.

Holiday Mittens
Art Center

Place at a center a supply of mitten cutouts. Also provide wrapping paper scraps, cotton balls, scissors, and glue. A child tears or cuts the wrapping paper and glues it to a mitten. She trims any paper hanging over the edges of the mitten, with help as needed. Then she embellishes her mitten with cotton balls.

Janet Kortright
St. Mary's Catholic Daycare/Preschool
Kenosha, WI

Letter and Number Lights
Literacy Center

Make a supply of lightbulb cutouts (pattern on page 283). Label half the bulbs with different letters and the remaining half with different numbers. Attach two separate lengths of yarn to a wall as shown; then attach a letter bulb to one length and a number bulb to the second length. Place the bulbs and a container of spring-style clothespins nearby. A child clips each bulb to the appropriate length.

Mary Robles
Milwaukie, OR

Pattern Prints
Math Center

Use holiday-related stamps to make several pattern strips. Place the pattern strips at a table along with the corresponding stamps, stamp pads, and blank paper strips. A youngster chooses a pattern strip. Then he uses the stamps to copy and extend the pattern on a blank strip.

Jennifer Schear
Clover Patch Preschool
Cedar Falls, IA

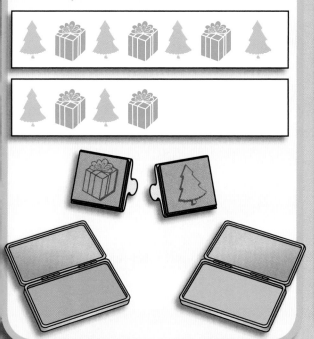

Spicy Reindeer
Sensory Center

Cut out a copy of the reindeer pattern on page 95. Use the resulting template to make a sandpaper reindeer for each child. Place the cutouts at a table along with a mixture of spices, such as ginger, ground cloves, and ground cinnamon. A youngster rubs his fingers over the sandpaper, feeling the texture. Then he brushes glue over the reindeer and sprinkles spices over the glue. If desired, he glues his reindeer to a sheet of contrasting paper.

Doreen James
Doreen's Kids Family Daycare
Pfafftown, NC

Kwanzaa Feast Mat
Fine-Motor Area

Place masking tape and brown construction paper at a center. A child attaches lengths of masking tape to a sheet of construction paper as shown. (Provide help as needed.) She rubs the side of an unwrapped brown crayon over the surface of the paper. Then she uses scissors to fringe-cut the ends of the paper.

Janet Boyce
Cokato, MN

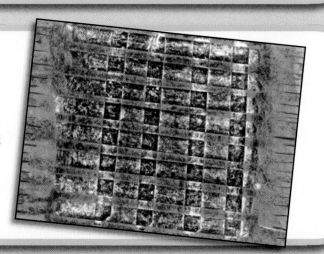

Learning Centers

Let's Look Inside!
Discovery Center

Got junk? Place a nonworking item—such as a tape recorder, a radio, or a clock—at a center along with safety goggles; tools such as screwdrivers, pliers, and magnifying glasses to investigate the item; and materials for recording observations. A student visits the center and dons the safety goggles. Then she uses the tools to take the item apart and investigates its inner parts. She writes her observations or dictates them for an adult to record.

Mileen McGee
George O. Barr School
Silvis, IL

H Is for *Heart*
Literacy Center

Make a supply of die-cut letters, including several *H* cutouts. Put the letters at a center near a supersize paper heart. A child visits the center and chooses a letter. If the letter is an *H,* she places it on the heart. If it is not, she places it to the side. She repeats the process with each remaining letter.

Mary Robles
Little Acorns Preschool
Milwaukie, OR

Rainbow Wrap
Play Dough Center

Place different-colored batches of play dough at a center along with several plastic knives. A visiting youngster flattens a ball of play dough into a disc. He places a different color of play dough in the center of the disc and then folds the disc over and flattens it again. He repeats the process with the remaining colors of dough. Finally, he rolls his dough into a cylindrical shape; then he uses a plastic knife to cut the dough in pieces, revealing a rainbow of colors inside!

Audra Meyerhofer
Long Beach, CA

Golden Treats
Math Center

To prepare, place a laminated pot cutout on a table along with a large die and a bowl of vanilla wafers (gold coins). A student rolls the die, counts the dots on top of the die, and then places the corresponding number of gold coins on the pot. When he reaches a predetermined number of coins, he receives a special snack of vanilla wafers!

adapted from an idea by Donna Stensland
Park Hill School
Syracuse, NY

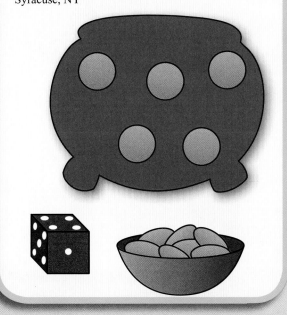

Woolly Lamb

Wonderful Wool
Art Center

Make a class supply of page 96. Put the pages at a center along with glue and a supply of shredded white paper. A youngster visits the center, crumples the paper shreds, and then glues them to a sheep to create its wool.

Carole Watkins
Holy Family Child Care
Crown Point, IN

Bakery Delight
Flannelboard Center

In advance, hot-glue felt to a cookie tin, allowing the lid to be removed so felt pieces can be stored inside. Put the resulting cake at a center with a supply of die-cut felt shapes and an apron. A child puts the apron on and pretends to be a baker decorating the mock cake with felt shapes.

Karen Tubbs
Malad Head Start
Malad, ID

Learning Centers

Tube Puppet
Art Center

Place brown paper lunch bags, newspaper strips, cardboard tubes, masking tape, markers, and glue at a table. Also provide a variety of collage materials. A child stuffs a bag with newspaper strips. Then he inserts a cardboard tube into the opening of the bag and tapes the bag to the tube with help as needed. Finally, he decorates his puppet as desired.

Sharon Whitfield
Davidson United Methodist Church Preschool
Davidson, NC

Kite Tails and Bow Ties
Math Center

To prepare, label each of several craft foam kites with a different number; then attach a tail to each kite. Place the kites at a center along with a supply of tinted bow-tie pasta. A youngster visits the center and identifies the number on a kite. Then she places the corresponding number of bow-tie pasta pieces on the kite tail. She continues in the same way with each remaining kite.

Margaret Ann Aumen
Emory United Methodist Nursery School
York Springs, PA

Cutting Carrots
Fine-Motor Area

Place a supply of orange construction paper strips (carrots) at a center. Provide scissors, a soup pot, a ladle, and a stuffed rabbit. A visiting child cuts a carrot into small pieces over the pot. Then he stirs the soup with the ladle and gives the bunny a taste. (If desired, use the pieces for future collage projects.)

Karen Amatrudo
Circle Nursery School
Madison, CT

Counting Bags
Math Center

Gather a variety of small items, such as plastic animals, shells, milk jug caps, and poker chips. Place the sets of objects in separate bags, varying the amounts. Put the bags at a center along with corresponding number cards. A child picks a bag, removes the items, and counts them aloud. Then she places the card with the corresponding number near the bag and puts the items back in the bag. She continues in the same way with each remaining bag.

adapted from an idea by Jen Goldman
Sol Feinstone Elementary
Newtown, PA

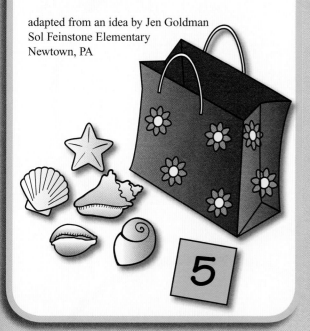

Let's Go Camping!
Dramatic-Play Area

Stock your dramatic-play area with a variety of camping-related items, such as a small dome tent, sleeping bags or blankets, working flashlights, a makeshift grill, a cooler, plastic food, plates, and cooking accessories. A youngster visits the area and uses the props to engage in pretend camping play.

Diane Kovac
Capital Area Intermediate Unit
Summerdale, PA

Patriotic Mosaics
Art Center

With permission, collect paint sample cards in shades of red, white, and blue from a home improvement store. Cut the sample cards into small squares and place them at a center along with a sheet of tagboard and glue. A student brushes glue over a portion of the tagboard. Then she places squares on the glue. She continues until she has covered the tagboard with patriotic colors.

Phyllis Prestridge
West Amory Elementary
Amory, MS

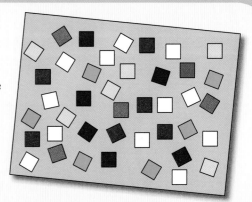

Pizza Topping Patterns
Use with "Pizza Patterns" on page 87.

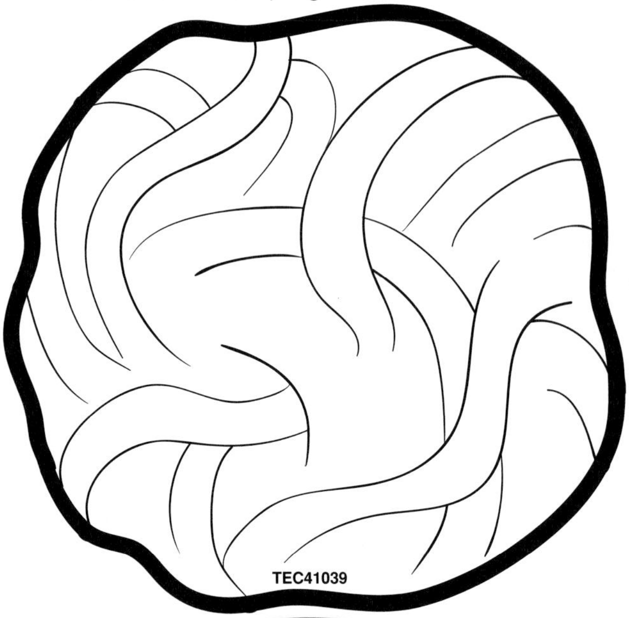

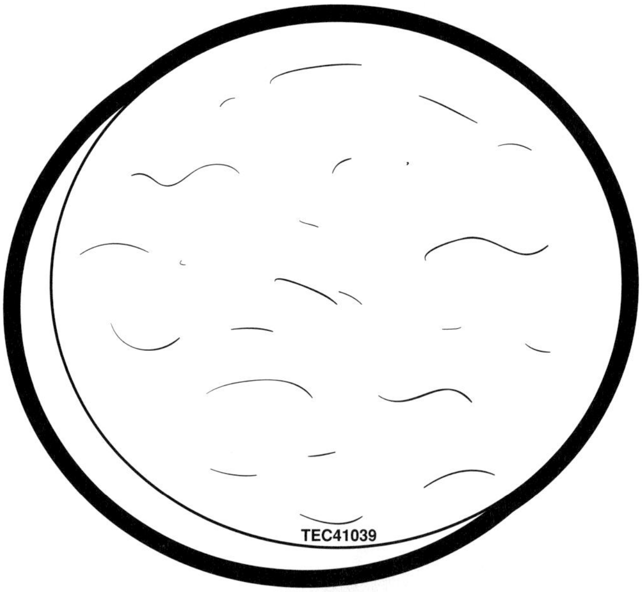

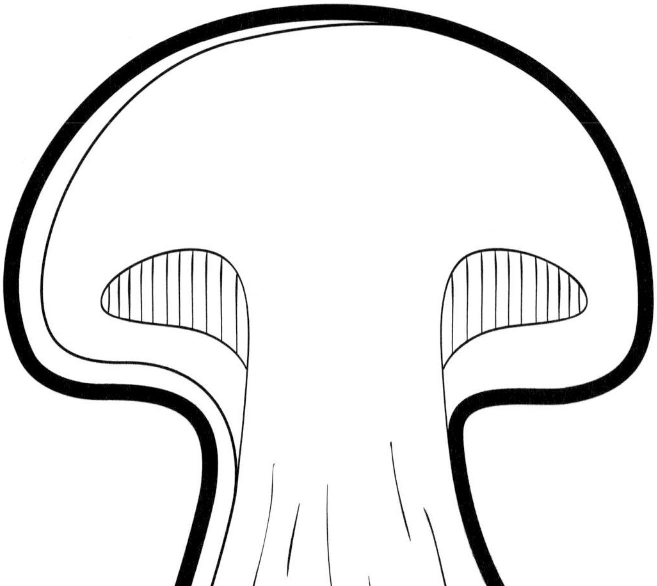

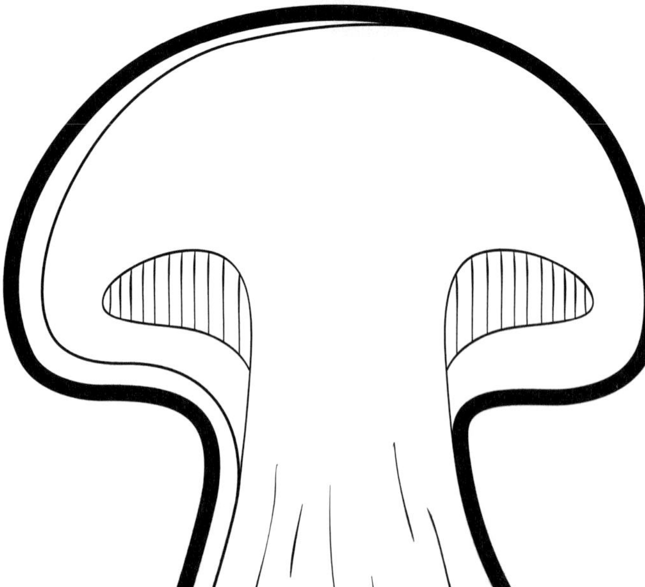

TEC41039

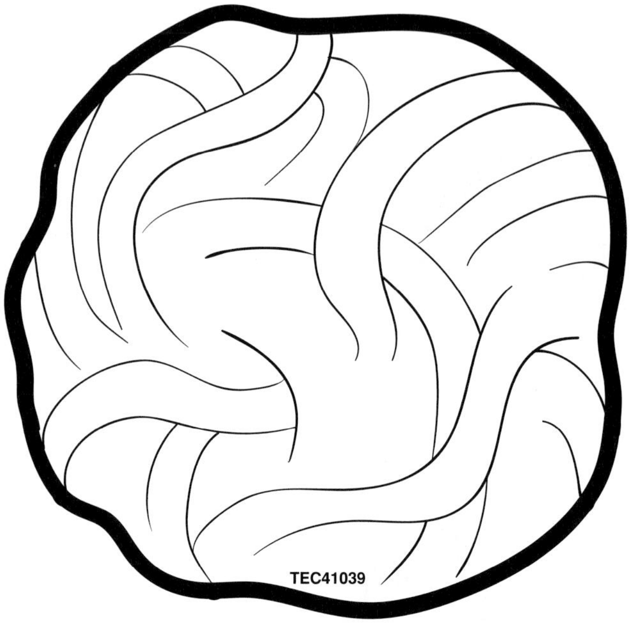

TEC41039

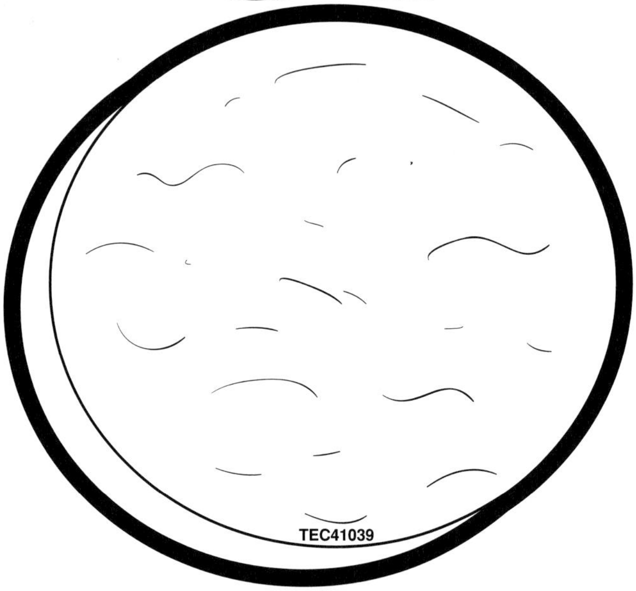

TEC41039

TEC41039

TEC41039

TEC41039

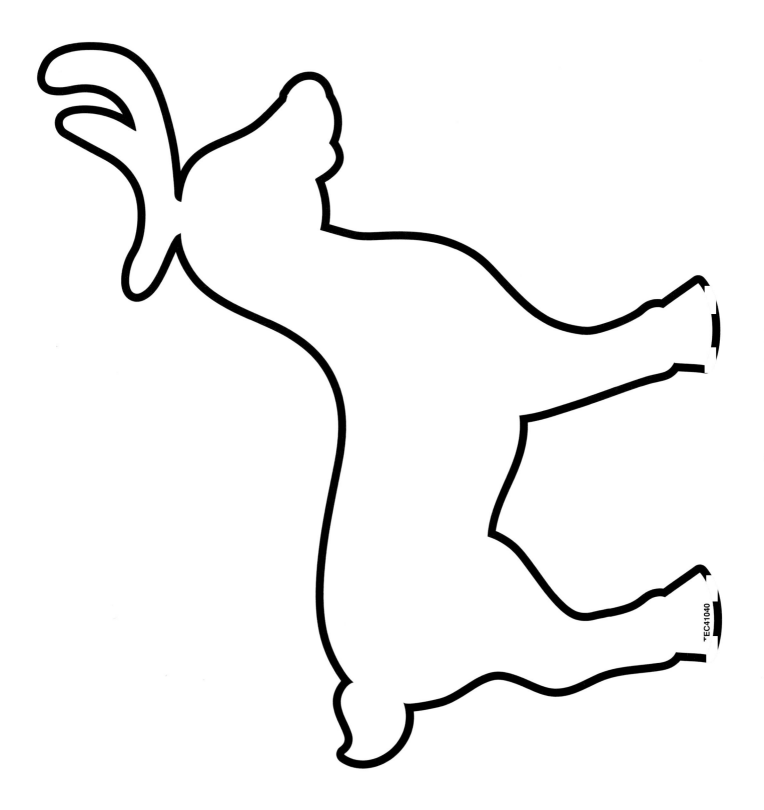

TEC41040

Woolly Lamb

Note to the teacher: Use with "Wonderful Wool" on page 91.

MANAGEMENT TIPS & TIMESAVERS

Management Tips & Timesavers

Circle-Time Clock

Youngsters keep track of circle-time activities with this unique prop! Divide a circle cutout as shown and label each section with a different circle-time activity. Attach a poster board arrow. Then have a different child move the arrow as youngsters complete each activity. *Peggy Carty, Tot Spot Childcare, Conroe, TX*

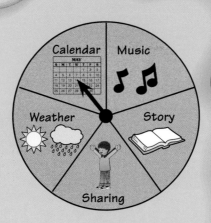

Watch Your Step

To help students walk quietly in line, tell them there are tomatoes on the floor. To keep from squashing the tomatoes, they must walk quietly and gently. Then invite youngsters to check their shoes when they arrive at their destination to make sure they did not step on any tomatoes. *Amy Fisk, Riverside, CA*

Apple Hunt

To get students settled after recess, post an apple cutout in your classroom. Youngsters come in from recess, put their things away, and look for the apple. When each child sees the apple, she sits in your circle-time area. Then, when everyone is seated, a student volunteer tells everyone where the apple is located. *Nicole Furfaro, St. Paul Catholic School, Guelph, Ontario, Canada*

Songs

 The Farmer in the Dell

 Bingo

 London Bridge

 The Itsy-Bitsy Spider

Choose a Song

Being the conductor may quickly become one of the most popular jobs in your class! Post a chart listing familiar class songs. Have your little conductor use a decorated dowel rod to point to a song he wishes to sing. Then invite him to help you lead the class in singing the song. *Kristin Przekota, Gladstone School, Chicago, IL*

Cleanup Song

Lead youngsters in singing this song to praise them for a successful classroom cleanup!

(sung to the tune of "The Farmer in the Dell")

We worked together today
To put our things away.
I'm proud I helped today
To keep our room so clean. Yay!

Management Tips & Timesavers

Beat the Buzzer

Motivate students to clean up quickly with this timely tip. Set a kitchen timer for five minutes and encourage students to have the room neat and tidy before the timer buzzes. After students successfully beat the buzzer a predetermined number of times, reward them with a special treat or privilege. *Sherry Palla, St. Paul's Lutheran School, Cannon Falls, MN*

Classroom Helper

Here's a nifty alternative to a job chart. Each morning select a youngster to be the Child of the Day. She does all the important jobs for that day, such as being calendar helper, line leader, and messenger. *Kelly Noll, Diamond Street Early Childhood Center, Akron, PA*

Less Mess

Minimize play dough mess by providing a plastic tray for each student at the center. The tray gives him a defined area in which to roll, cut, and mold his play dough masterpiece. *Mary Bleasdale, R. E. Davis Elementary School, Sumter, SC*

Color-Coded Centers

To prevent overcrowding at centers, color-code your centers and obtain matching inexpensive plastic bracelets. Have each student choose a bracelet and go to the corresponding center. When all the bracelets of one color have been taken, the students know that center is full. *Kay L. Muehlberger, Good Shepherd Christian Nursery School, Easton, PA*

Sitting Quietly

This cute reminder is an easy way to help students prepare for circle time. Simply cover your eyes and say, "Surprise me!" Have little ones rush to quietly sit in their spots. Then uncover your eyes, give them a big smile, and thank them for the wonderful surprise! *Phyllis Johnson, Opelousas Head Start Academy, Opelousas, LA*

Management Tips & Timesavers

Center Time Books

Here's a simple way to incorporate literacy in your centers! Obtain several inexpensive napkin holders. Slide books related to the center theme in the holders and then place each holder at the appropriate center. *Linda Dammann, Immanuel Lutheran School, Columbus, NE*

Silver Lining

Use a silver marker to trace patterns or write prompts on black paper. The silver lines are eye-catching and easy for you or your little ones to follow when cutting. *Kathleen Root, Hope Ridge U.M. Preschool, Mentor, OH*

Name ___Celina R.___

1	2	3	4	5	6	7	8	9	10
11	12	13	14	15	16	17	18	19	20
21	22	23	24	25	26	27	28	29	30
31	32	33	34	35	36	37	38	39	40
41	42	43	44	45	46	47	48	49	50
51	52	53	54	55	56	57	58	59	60
61	62	63	64	65	66	67	68	69	70
71	72	73	74	75	76	77	78	79	80
81	82	83	84	85	86	87	88	89	90
91	92	93	94	95	96	97	98	99	100

Time to Tidy

Instead of singing a cleanup song, try using a recorded song to designate when it's time to clean up! Assign a recorded song as your class cleanup song. Then simply press play, and youngsters will know that it's time to clean up and get ready for the next activity. *Ruth Dorsch, Zion Lutheran Preschool, Fairmont, OK*

Count on It

Here's a simple way to keep a running record of a youngster's counting skills. Personalize a hundred chart for each child. The first time you assess a child's counting, color the squares to the number she reaches. Each subsequent time you assess her, continue coloring squares using different crayon colors. *Karen Eiben, The Learning House Preschool, La Salle, IL*

A Friendly Reminder

To motivate youngsters to line up quickly as well as correctly, try this tip! Tell students to look at the classmate in front of them in line. If the child isn't standing in line correctly, prompt the youngster to gently tap his classmate on the shoulder. You'll be surprised at how fast your little ones will be lined up and ready to go! *Anita McManus, Christ Church Preschool and Kindergarten, Charlotte, NC*

Management Tips & Timesavers

Sharing Success

Little ones can't wait to "fly" these nifty kites home. Display a personalized kite for each child. Whenever a youngster accomplishes a goal, write it on a bow cutout and attach it to the kite's tail. Add a new bow to the tail each time another goal is mastered. *Tammy M. Davis, Casey-Westfield School, Charleston, IL*

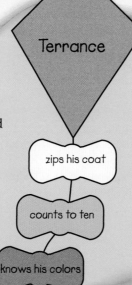

Terrance

zips his coat

counts to ten

knows his colors

Silly Stories

Try this tip to keep youngsters' attention during storytime. Choose a story with entertaining characters. As you read the story aloud, substitute students' names for the characters' names throughout the book. Little ones are focused as they eagerly listen for their names. *Kimberly Bass, Condell Intergenerational Day Center, Libertyville, IL*

Zipped Lips

This humorous prop is a fun way to remind students of quiet time. Cut a pair of lips from a piece of heavy paper. Then glue the fabric edges of a zipper to the lips. The zipper should still be able to zip and unzip. When it's important that youngsters be quiet, such as when walking down the hall, hold up the lips and zip them. *Carolyn Bryant, Richmond Day Nursery, Richmond, IN*

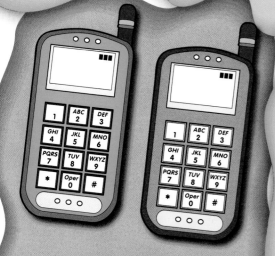

Work It Out

Simple props are sometimes all it takes to help students solve a misunderstanding. Place two nonoperational cellular phones in a small basket. When a minor disagreement arises between two students, give each one a phone. Help them take turns using the phones to discuss the disagreement and the best way to solve it. *Lois Caplin Provost, Warwick, MA*

Corner Safety

Use Velcro fasteners to attach novelty erasers to the corners of furniture. The erasers soften the corners and prevent bumps. Plus youngsters love the colorful eraser options! *Evon Rose Todd, Mid Cities Head Start, Euless, TX*

Management Tips & Timesavers

A Tidy Song

Encourage youngsters to clean your classroom centers with this sing-along. *Cari Charron, School District 28 Strong Start Centre, Quesnel, British Columbia, Canada*

(sung to the tune of "This Old Man")

Clean up, girls. Clean up, boys.
Clean up all the blocks and toys.
Don't forget the dishes and the cups.
That's the way we all clean up.

Good Visions

To make a pair of good-choice glasses, simply embellish a pair of nonprescription glasses. Tell little ones that when you wear the glasses, you can see only the youngsters who are making good choices. To redirect students who are not making good choices, say, "Oh, I think my glasses are dirty!" Clean them with a tissue and then put them back on. No doubt youngsters will have modified their behavior. *Jennifer Kisleiko, Kaleidoscope Head Start at Settlement Music School, Philadelphia, PA*

Find Your Seat

To shake up circle-time seating as well as promote letter recognition, label each circle-time spot with a different letter card. Then set a basket containing matching letter cards near your circle-time area. Have each student take a letter from the basket and sit on the matching circle-time spot. *Staci Peterson, Voyager Elementary, Alexandria, MN*

Sparkling Clean

Here's a quick way to tidy up a glitter spill. Simply roll a ball of play dough over the spill to pick up the glitter. Then squish the ball to mix the glitter with the play dough. Place the sparkling dough at a center for students to use. *Karen Padgett, Waycross, GA*

Quiet Hallways

Before little ones leave your classroom, invite each youngster to place an imaginary bubble in her mouth. Encourage little ones to keep the bubbles in their mouths until they reach their destination. Change this tip by switching the bubble to another object, like a butterfly, sock, or kitchen sink! *April Grills, Kensington School, Naperville, IL*

OUR READERS WRITE

Our Readers Write

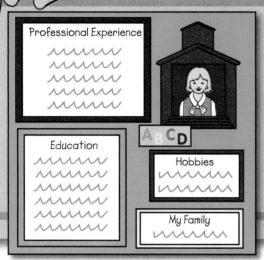

Meet Your Teacher

To introduce myself at our open house, I post scrapbook pages with photos and information about my education, hobbies, goals for the year, family, and work experience. I've always received many compliments from parents about this display.

Sarah Booth
Messiah Nursery School
South Williamsport, PA

Time to Pack

I use this simple call-and-answer song to signal to each youngster when it's his turn to pack his things at the end of the day.

(sung to the tune of "Where Is Thumbkin?")

Teacher: Where is [child's name]?
Where is [child's name]?
Child: Here I am! Here I am!   *The child stands.*
Class: How are you today, [sir/miss]?
Child: Very well. I thank you.
Class: Walk away! Walk away!   *The child leaves to pack.*

Wendy Fitzgerald
Grenfell Elementary Community School
Grenfell, Saskatchewan, Canada

An Apple a Day

To count to the 100th day of school, I post a large apple tree cutout in a location that is easily accessible to students. Each day a student adds a numbered apple to the tree. When we reach the 100th day of school, we celebrate by having a big apple party, complete with apple pie and ice cream.

Dorothy Murfin
Live Oak Preschool
Athens, GA

Birthday Headbands

Instead of making a birthday crown for each child for his birthday, I make a simple birthday headband. I purchase star-studded garland from our local dollar store. Then I form a piece of garland into a circular shape and place it on the birthday child's head. My youngsters always love their shiny birthday headbands.

Sarah Booth

Monthly Placemats

I found a simple way to reinforce skills during snacktime and lunch. Every month I have each student make a placemat. I laminate the placemats and then use a permanent marker to program each placemat with letters, numbers, or personal information such as the child's address and phone number. Throughout mealtime I ask youngsters questions about the information on their placemats.

Erin Rutter
Northview Preschool
Dayton, OH

Helping Hands

To give youngsters an opportunity to earn a classroom pet, I send home hand cutouts. When a youngster uses his helping hands at home, a parent writes the child's action on a hand cutout and then the youngster brings it to school to be displayed on our "Helping Hands" board. When we reach a predetermined number of cutouts, I purchase two new fish for our fish tank.

Monica Dasilva
Eldon B. Keith School
Brockton, MA

Picture Magnets

When picture time rolls around at my school, I use this tip to protect youngsters' wallet-size photos. I gather several baseball card sleeves and hot-glue a magnet to the back of each one. Then I slide a photo into each sleeve and display the photos on the cabinet in my classroom. Youngsters love to see their photos displayed!

Melissa Rose
Early Childhood Alliance
Fort Wayne, IN

Class Donations

To make a class wish list, I glue a picture of each desired item to a different index card and then label each card with the item's price and the place where it can be purchased. I punch a hole in each card and put all the cards on a binder ring. When a parent wishes to donate an item to our class, she looks through the cards to select an item and then removes the item's card from the ring. I get many wonderful books and toys using this idea.

Missy Goldenberg
Beth Shalom Preschool
Overland Park, KS

The Birthday Book

To make this book, I cut apart an inexpensive month chart and attach each month to a different sheet of construction paper. On each page, I glue photos of the birthday girls and boys for that month. Then, beside each photo, I write the student's name and his birthday. I laminate all the pages and bind them together with a cover. My youngsters love to look at this birthday book!

Vanessa Levin
Carrollton Elementary
Carrollton, TX

Our Readers Write

Wonderful Webs

To preserve an abandoned spiderweb, I spray both sides of the web with white spray paint. Then I quickly place a dark sheet of paper on the web. The web sticks to the paper, which makes it easy to take down. When the web and paper are dry, I place them in a plastic sheet protector. I then invite youngsters to feel and observe the web.

Tammy Wetzel
Canterbury Preschool
Mountain Brook, AL

Naptime Fun

To make rest time more enjoyable for my youngsters I have a few special sleeping spots in my classroom. These spots are fun places around the room that youngsters particularly enjoy, such as our reading couch or next to our giant teddy bear. Each day I invite a different student to sleep in each special spot.

Cindy Kelly
St. Bernard School
Wabash, IN

Color Mix Magic

I found a fun way to teach little ones about mixing colors. I attach two clean potato chip containers bottom to bottom and cover the resulting tube with paper. Before students arrive I place a large purple pom-pom in one end of the tube. At circle time, youngsters watch as I place a red and blue pom-pom in the opposite end of the tube. While I shake the tube to "mix" the colors, I switch ends. To the amazement of my children, when I open the tube, I remove the purple pom-pom!

Elizabeth Mowery
Moravian Child Care Center
Gnadenhutten, OH

Puppet Pals

I have a great tip for getting a large supply of puppets for a small amount of money. I purchase inexpensive stuffed animals. (Many of mine came from garage sales.) Then I simply slit open the bottom and remove the stuffing from the body area. Because the material curls inward when it is cut, there is no need to hem it!

Diane L. Flohr
Orchard Trails Elementary
Kent City, MI

An Expression of Thanks

The firefighters at our local fire station love this unique thank-you card. I make a supersize dalmatian cutout, without spots. After I copy student photos and cut out their faces, I randomly glue the faces on the dalmatian to make the spots. This cute project would also make a fun fire prevention display!

Kathy Hurford
Tri-Cap Head Start
Booneville, IN

Thumbs-Up!

This simple visual reminder helps my youngsters hold their scissors correctly. When my students hold their scissors I remind them to look at their thumbs. If their thumbs are pointing at the ceiling, then the students are ready to cut.

Shannon Van Dyk
Children's Garden
Sparta, NJ

What a Day!

To end my youngsters' day on a positive note, I ask each child to tell me the best part of his day before he gets ready to leave. It helps everyone end the day with a big smile!

Lola Anderson
Canby Head Start
Canby, MN

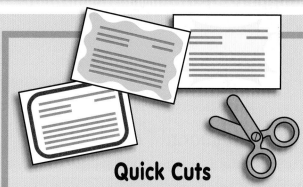

Quick Cuts

This quick activity is a great way to recycle while helping my little ones practice their cutting skills. I gather extra subscription cards from magazines and place them in a container with scissors. Youngsters cut the cards into several pieces. The cards are perfect for this activity because they are thicker than regular paper and are easy for little hands to hold.

Dena Stansbury
Grace Children's Learning Center
Manassas, VA

Sweet Treats

My youngsters love these cute treat cups! For each child, I glue together the bottoms of two clear plastic cups. I have students paint the cups as shown and then add facial details. For a final touch, I write "Got Treats?" with a white gel pen on the bottom cup.

Bonnie Martin
Hopewell Country Day School
Pennington, NJ

Our Readers Write

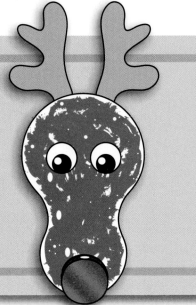

Rudolph's Nose

To make this cute window decoration, I have each youngster sponge-paint a simple reindeer head cutout with a hole cut in the nose area. When the paint is dry, I help each child attach eye and antler cutouts to the reindeer head. Then I tape a disc-shaped sucker to the back of the reindeer so the edible portion is in the opening and it resembles Rudolph's nose.

Jennie Jensen
North Cedar Elementary
Mechanicsville, IA

Seasonal Parachutes

Instead of using a parachute for many group activities, I use a seasonal vinyl tablecloth. My youngsters particularly enjoy games in which we place foam balls or foam cutouts on the tablecloth and then shake the tablecloth until all the items have landed on the floor. My little ones scramble to collect and count the balls, and then we play another round.

Karen Eiben
The Learning House Preschool
LaSalle, IL

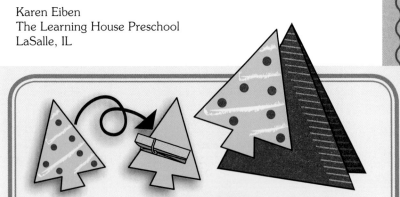

Family Gifts

To make a set of seasonal napkin holders, I give each student a holiday cutout for each person in her family and invite her to decorate the cutouts as desired. Then I have her glue each cutout to a wooden clothespin. When each resulting holder is dry, I instruct her to clip a folded napkin in it.

Pennye Pucheu
Alice Boucher Elementary
Lafayette, LA

"Scent-sational" Trees

I have each child use air-dry clay to make a peak at the top of a pull-up air freshener. When the clay is dry, I have her paint the top portion of the air freshener green and the bottom portion red. Then I invite her to embellish her tree with pom-poms, foam shapes, pipe cleaners, and miniature garland. I receive a lot of compliments on this cute project!

Bonnie Martin
Hopewell Country Day School
Pennington, NJ

Adorable Dreidel Costumes

When my youngsters perform "I Have a Little Dreidel," they each wear the simple dreidel costume shown. I attach a cardboard tube to a painted disposable plate to make a hat. Then I attach yarn to the hat and to a painted poster board dreidel. I slip the dreidel over the child's head and tie the hat in place under the youngster's chin.

Missy Goldenberg
Beth Shalom Nursery School
Overland Park, KS

Block Wall of Fame

To preserve students' block creations, I designate an area of the classroom wall to be the Block Wall of Fame. When a student builds a special structure, I take a photo of her with the creation and post it on the board along with a caption dictated by the child.

Karen Guess
St. Richard's School
Indianapolis, IN

Quiet Chairs

Many students in my class are sensitive to noise. To help these youngsters, I collect a supply of used tennis balls from a local fitness center and use a utility knife to cut an X in each ball. Then I slide a ball on the end of each chair leg. When students move the chairs, they quietly glide across the floor.

Heather Nucifora
Palmer Elementary
Easton, PA

A Snack for Birds

To make this peanut butter–free bird treat, I have students place water and birdseed in a small empty milk jug. Next, I slide a yarn hanger into the carton and then put the carton in the freezer. When the water is frozen, I cut away the carton and hang the treat outside.

Ya-Fen Yen
MIT Lincoln Lab Children's Center
Lexington, MA

WILSON

Super Bowl Stars

After the two teams who will play in the Super Bowl are determined, I have each child decorate a personalized team jersey cutout to match the team he believes will win. After the Super Bowl is played, we discuss the results and count how many students were rooting for the winning team.

Marni Driessen
Fontenelle Elementary
Omaha, NE

Our Readers Write

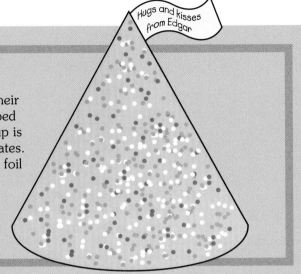

Hugs and kisses from Edgar

A Valentine Kiss

My youngsters love making this special holiday treat for their families. I instruct each student to brush glue on a cone-shaped paper cup and then roll the cup in silver glitter. When the cup is dry, I have him fill it with Hershey's Hugs and Kisses chocolates. Then I help him cover the bottom of the cup with aluminum foil and attach a paper strip with a personal message.

adapted from an idea by Claudia Summers
Jack and Jill Preschool
Leavenworth, KS

Copy This

Use a digital camera to give youngsters' eyes and hands a workout. I take photos of wonderful creations that students make in the play dough and block centers. Then I print the photos and encourage students to use them to help in rebuilding the creations!

Barbara Chapman
Fiddlesticks Cooperative Preschool
Centralia, WA

Stories by Seuss

During the week of Dr. Seuss's birthday, I read several of his stories to my students. At the end of the week, I write the name of each child's favorite story on a separate white paper strip. Then I have him add an illustration to his strip. Finally, I attach the strips to a supersize red hat cutout and mount the hat to a wall in my classroom.

adapted from an idea by Melinda Alves
Agawam Early Childhood Center
Agawam, MA

Green Eggs and Ham

Stories From Home

I send home with each student a blank cassette tape and a letter asking parents to record themselves reading their child's favorite story. Each day, I play a tape at the beginning of naptime while little ones are getting settled.

Renee Brown, New Adventure Learning Center, Brevard, NC

Our Readers Write

Critter Cruisers

To make one of these cute cars, I cover an empty tissue box with paper. Then I attach tagboard wheels to the car. During center time, I set out the cars along with several stuffed toys. My little ones love to "drive" their favorite toys around the room.

Donna Foss
Little People of Southbury
Southbury, CT

Charge It

I reuse the sample cards that come in credit card applications. I place the cards in my grocery store center, and youngsters use them to "purchase" the groceries!

Cheryl Gort
Fantasy Farm Child Development Center
Spokane, WA

Egg in a Nest

For this Easter-themed take-home treat, I give each student a ball of raised bread dough and have him form a nest. Then I help him dip an uncooked egg in tinted water before having him place the egg in the nest. Finally, I let the dough rise again, and then I bake the egg and nest at 325 degrees for about 35 minutes.

Nancy Morgan
Care-A-Lot In-Home Daycare and Preschool
Bremerton, WA

A Mother's Day Tea

I've received many compliments on my annual Mother's Day tea. During the party my little ones perform songs and poems. Then each student shares a plate of goodies with his mother or other special woman as I serve the tea and juice. To end the celebration, the children sit in a circle with their moms and play a version of Hot Potato called Hugs and Kisses. As music plays, students pass a paper heart around the circle. When the music stops, the child holding the heart gives his mom a hug and a kiss.

Charlene Macdonald
Kid's Country Child Care and Learning Center
Hanson, MA

Our Readers Write

Personal Gardens

Before a planting activity, take youngsters on a nature walk and have them select interesting rocks and twigs. Have each child plant seeds in a small bowl and then arrange the found items on his garden for a personal touch. If desired, allow each child to choose small plastic figures, such as dinosaurs or farm animals, to add to his garden as well.

Deborah Ryan
Milwaukie, OR

Bunny Olympics

I combine an Easter celebration with a gross-motor workout with the Bunny Olympics! My students carry carrots during a relay race, wear bunny-ear headbands during a hopping contest, and play egg toss with plastic eggs. At the end of the Bunny Olympics, I present each child with a certificate and a medal.

Carol Allen
Harvest Christian Preschool
Griffin, GA

Our Tree

We celebrate Earth Day by designating a tree on our playground as the Preschool Tree. Whenever we go outside, we gather around the tree and sing a song. We also spend time discussing what type of tree we've chosen and how trees are important. Finally, I take a photo of each child next to the tree.

Suzanne Foote
East Ithaca Preschool
Ithaca, NY

Even ten little fingers
Can't count the ways
You care for me
Each and every day.

Happy Mother's Day!
Love,
Sammy
May 8, 2009

Mom

A Card for Mom

To make this adorable keepsake, I accordion-fold a 6" x 18" piece of paper for each student. I write the text at the beginning and end of the card. Then I have each child make handprints and attach a photo to the interior of the card as shown.

Toni L. Adams
Learning Together Family Literacy, Inc.
Holmen, WI

Sign a Song

Whenever I sing familiar songs with my little ones, I use American Sign Language to sign the key words. After several repetitions, my youngsters begin to imitate the signs. Eventually, singing and signing becomes natural to them!

Karen Favor
Harold Holliday Montessori
Kansas City, MO

Our Readers Write

Making S'mores

In my dramatic-play area, I create a pretend campfire using cardboard tubes and paper. Then I attach a cotton ball (marshmallow) to each of several sticks. I also set out extra cotton balls along with light and dark brown paper squares (graham crackers and chocolate). A child pretends to roast a marshmallow and then uses the other materials to make a s'more of his own.

Eva Parker
Tender Care Learning Centers
Clairton, PA

Doughnuts With Dad

Help little ones celebrate Father's Day with this simple idea. I invite each youngster's dad (or other special man) to join us one morning for doughnuts. When everyone is finished munching on doughnuts, the little ones perform a song and poem.

Kellie Roane
Gulf Breeze Community Preschool
Gulf Breeze, FL

Oodles of Noodles

Here's an inexpensive way to make manipulatives with a variety of uses. I purchase several swimming noodles and cut them into pieces of different lengths. The resulting manipulatives can be stacked to make patterns, strung onto a large rope, or used as blocks. The possibilities are endless!

Pauline Rodriguez
Little People's Preschool
Union City, CA

Summertime Creations

For this art project, I fill summer-themed candy molds with plaster of paris. I tap the molds to remove any air bubbles. After the plaster is mostly dry, I remove it from the cast to finish drying. The students decorate the casts with markers, tempera paints, and glitter glue. Then I add a magnet or pin to the back of each cast.

Diane L. Flohr
Orchard Trails Elementary
Kent City, MI

Neat Treats

Here's a great way to keep little ones' hands clean while they eat ice pops. I cut off the top of a small paper cup and cut a small slit in the bottom of the cup. Then I push the ice pop stick through the slit. The cup catches the messy drips!

Lori Longtin
Little Creations Preschool
Sherman, TX

Ocean Decorations

I found that a recycled shower curtain with an ocean-themed print is a great source of reuseable decorations. I cut fish and sea creatures from the curtain and use them to decorate bulletin boards and student art displays. I also use the fish as cubby tags!

Missy Goldenberg
Beth Shalom Preschool
Overland Park, KS

Birthday Bucket

To celebrate youngsters' birthdays, I stock a large plastic sand bucket with a supply of inexpensive toys and place a plastic shovel nearby. On each child's birthday I invite her to scoop a treat from the bucket.

Cindy Kelly
St. Bernard School
Wabash, IN

Unforgettable Memories

This memento reminds little ones of our time together for years to come. I type the poem shown and print a copy for each child on floral paper. Then I sign my name on each copy and attach a packet of forget-me-not seeds.

Sarah Booth
Messiah Nursery School
South Williamsport, PA

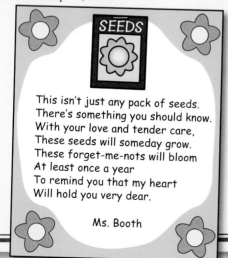

SEEDS

This isn't just any pack of seeds.
There's something you should know.
With your love and tender care,
These seeds will someday grow.
These forget-me-nots will bloom
At least once a year
To remind you that my heart
Will hold you very dear.

Ms. Booth

We'll always "bee" friends!

"Bee-utiful" Shirts

To make these wearable keepsakes, I put a piece of poster board inside each shirt and use a black fabric marker to label it as shown. Then I have each youngster dip a potato half in yellow fabric paint and make a print on his shirt for himself and each of his classmates. When the shirts are dry, I invite each child to add bee features to a print on each shirt. Then I write each youngster's name below his bee.

Ada Goren
Winston-Salem, NC

SCIENCE EXPLORATIONS

Science Explorations

Will It Bounce?
Youngsters investigate a variety of items to test whether the items will bounce.

Materials:
feather
ball of aluminum foil
Silly Putty compound, molded into a ball
toy ball
copy of the recording sheet on page 121
    for each child

STEP 1
Ask little ones what it means when something bounces. After they share their thoughts, encourage them to stand and bounce up and down. Then have the youngsters take their seats. Invite them to name items they have seen bounce.

STEP 2
Present the feather, aluminum foil, Silly Putty compound, and ball. Ask youngsters to share which items they believe will bounce and which items will not bounce.

STEP 3
Give each youngster a recording sheet and a crayon. Drop the feather onto a tabletop and have students determine whether it bounced. If it bounced, have children color the corresponding picture. If not, have them leave the picture blank. Continue in the same way with each remaining item.

STEP 4
Ask students to determine which item was the best bouncer and which was the worst. Then encourage them to share why they believe certain items bounce better than others.

What Now?
Place a container of items at a center. You might consider including items such as an empty soda bottle, a plastic animal toy, a paper ball, and a small cardboard box. Encourage youngsters to visit the center and test the items to see whether any of them bounce.

Science Explorations

Living and Nonliving

Youngsters investigate the characteristics of living things with this exploration.

Materials:
doll
copy of page 122 for each child

STEP 1

Ask youngsters whether they can jump up and down. After they respond, have them jump up and down and then take their seats. Then explain that your doll can jump up and down as well. Make the doll jump up and down. Repeat the process with several different actions, such as dancing and clapping.

STEP 2

Next, ask youngsters whether they eat food and drink water. When they confirm that they do, ask them whether the doll eats and drinks as well. Lead students to conclude that the doll does not need food and water because it is not alive.

STEP 3

Ask students whether they grow. Invite youngsters to talk about how small they were as babies and how tall they are currently. Then ask whether the doll grows as well. Lead youngsters to conclude that the doll does not grow because it is not alive.

STEP 4

Ask youngsters to name other things that are alive and not alive. Then give each child a copy of page 122. Help her fold the minibooklet appropriately and then circle the pictures that identify living things.

What Now?

Help youngsters compare a real potted plant with an artificial potted plant. Prompt them to identify the parts of the plants. Then lead them to conclude that the real plant is alive and needs water and sunshine to grow and that the artificial plant is not alive and does not need water and sunshine.

Science Explorations

Frosty Fun
Youngsters explore frost with this wintry investigation!

Materials:
large tin can (smooth edges)
crushed ice
salt
jumbo craft stick
copy of page 123 for each child (optional)

STEP 1

On a chilly morning, take youngsters outside and have them notice the frost on trees, grass, and cars. If you live in a warmer climate, share pictures of frost with your students.

STEP 2

Tell students that they can make frost right in the classroom. Have youngsters help you place ice and salt in the can. Then instruct children to use the craft stick to stir the mixture.

STEP 3

As youngsters stir, encourage them to notice that the outside is turning white with frost. Encourage youngsters to touch the frost and describe how it feels.

STEP 4

If desired, give each child a copy of page 123. Help each youngster brush glue on the cover and on each booklet page. Then have him sprinkle iridescent glitter over the glue so it resembles frost. When the glue is dry, follow the directions shown to fold the booklet.

What Now?
To remind youngsters of their frost investigation, have each child complete the art project on page 10 titled "It's Frosty!"

118

Science Explorations

Sugar, Sugar
Fascinate your youngsters with this sweet and simple investigation!

Materials:
sugar cubes
shallow pan
tinted water
copy of page 124 for each child

STEP 1
Have students tell what they know about sugar. Explain that people buy loose grains of sugar in a bag but they can also buy sugar in cubes. Present a sugar cube and have students study and describe it.

STEP 2
Next, have students help you arrange sugar cubes in the pan to form a pyramid.

STEP 3
Ask youngsters what they think will happen to the cubes if you pour the tinted water into the pan. After several youngsters share their thoughts, pour the water into the pan. Then have students observe as the water rushes from the bottom of the pyramid to the top.

STEP 4
Give each child a copy of page 124. Encourage each youngster to color the sugar cubes to show what they look like after you poured the water into the pan.

What Now?
Remind youngsters that the water moved from the bottom of the sugar cube pyramid to the top. Help youngsters perform a similar test with paper towel strips. Have a child dip the end of a paper towel strip in tinted water and observe as the water moves up the strip.

119

Science Explorations

Too Much Treasure!

How many treasure chests will it take to sink these pirate ships? Your youngsters find out with this sink-and-float investigation!

idea by Maureen E. Cesari, Raleigh, NC

Materials:
2 foam trays, trimmed to make a large and small boat shape (pirate ships)
block manipulatives (treasure chests)
water table or tub of water

STEP 1

Show students the pirate ships. Have a volunteer place the small ship in the water. Then encourage youngsters to notice that the ship floats.

STEP 2

Tell students that the pirates have found a lot of treasure and need to put it on this ship. Show youngsters the treasure chests. Then ask each student to predict how many treasure chests can be placed on the boat without it sinking.

STEP 3

Have children carefully place treasure chests on the boat as you lead them in counting the chests aloud. Have youngsters stop when the boat begins to sink. Then have them compare the number of treasure chests on the boat to their predictions.

STEP 4

Repeat the process with the larger pirate ship, having students compare the number of chests placed on that boat to the number of chests placed on the smaller boat.

What Now?

Place a different treasure, such as jumbo play coins or washers, near the boats and tub of water. Have students repeat the experiment with the new treasure.

Does It Bounce?

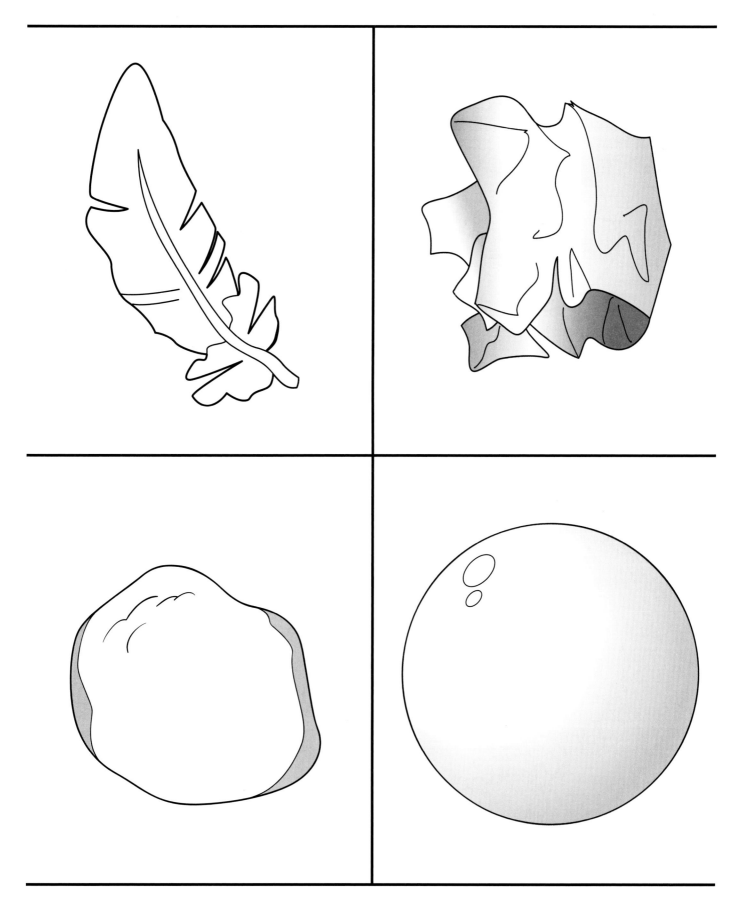

Which one is alive?

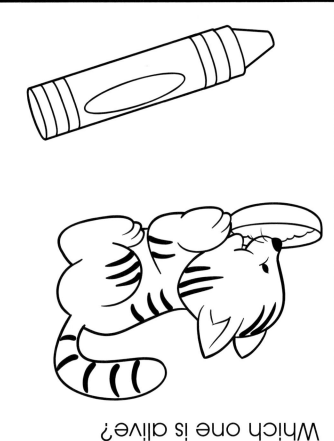

Which one is alive?

Which one is alive?

Living or Nonliving?

Name _____

Fold-and-Go Booklet: To make a booklet, cut on the bold line. Fold along the thin horizontal line (keeping the programming to the outside) and then fold along the thin vertical line (keeping the cover to the outside). Have each child point to or circle the living object on each page of his booklet.

Frost on the grass.

1

I See the Frost.

by _____

Frost on the leaves.

2

Frost on the car.

3

Note to the teacher: To make a booklet, cut on the bold line. Fold along the thin horizontal line (keeping the programming to the outside) and then fold along the thin vertical line (keeping the cover to the outside).

What Happened?

©The Mailbox® • TEC41041 • Feb./Mar. 2009

Note to the teacher: Use with "Sugar, Sugar" on page 119.

Songs & Such

SONGS & SUCH

To Preschool!

Welcome youngsters to preschool by leading them in several rounds of this catchy little ditty!

(sung to the tune of "A-hunting We Will Go")

To preschool we will go.
To preschool we will go.
We'll sing and play and laugh all day.
To preschool we will go!

To preschool we will go.
To preschool we will go.
We'll paint and glue and make friends too.
To preschool we will go!

LeeAnn Collins
Sunshine House Preschool
Lansing, MI

CLAP!

Clap, Slap, Tap, Lap

Use this quick-and-easy chant to get youngsters' attention and to quiet wiggly hands! Lead youngsters in performing the chant. During the final line, reduce your speaking volume until the final "lap" is said in a whisper.

Clap, clap, clap, clap.   *Clap hands.*
Slap, slap, slap, slap.   *Slap legs.*
Tap, tap, tap, tap.   *Tap hands on head.*
Lap, lap, lap, lap.   *Lay hands in lap.*

Melanie Marie Hays
Crossgates Methodist Children's Center
Brandon, MS

Five Red Apples

Youngsters are sure to enjoy this "tree-mendously" fun rhyme! Lead youngsters in reciting the rhyme five times, reducing the number of apples each time.

[Five] red apple(s) high in a tree.
Apples always taste so good to me!
So I shake that tree; one falls to the ground—CRUNCH!
Now there are [four] red apples, juicy and round.

Tammy Block
Church on the Hill Child Care Center
Norco, CA

Preschool Friends

Help students identify their names with this friendly song! Gather name cards. Then hold up a card and lead youngsters in singing the song. Help the student whose name card you're holding identify his name. Then repeat the process for each remaining card.

(sung to the tune of "The Farmer in the Dell")

Who is my preschool friend?
Who is my preschool friend?
Look, see—who could this be?
Who is my preschool friend?

Dodie Lowery
Creative Learning Center
Springfield, MO

Let's Clean Up!

Lead students in this toe-tapping song as they clean the room after center time.

(sung to the tune of "The More We Get Together")

Oh we can work together, together, together;
Oh we can work together to clean up this room.
Pick this up and that up and this up and that up.
Oh we can work together to clean up this room.

Deborah Patrick
Park Forest Elementary
State College, PA

It's Naptime

With this soothing song, youngsters are sure to be ready for a relaxing naptime. Lead students in singing the song slowly several times, getting quieter with each repetition. Then, when youngsters are settled in, play a recording of soothing naptime music.

(sung to the tune of "Head and Shoulders")

Head and shoulders, knees and toes (arms and fingers);
Head and shoulders, knees and toes (arms and fingers).
All of me is on top of my mat.
All of me is laying down—nice and flat!

Jodi Lee McNamara
Kids 'R' Kids
Lawrenceville, GA

SONGS & SUCH

Dancing Leaves

This simple fall action rhyme is perfect for even the youngest preschoolers!

Leaves are drifting softly down.

Slowly lower self to floor.

They make a carpet on the ground.

Lie on the floor.

Then swish—the wind comes whistling by

Swing arms and stand.

And sends them dancing to the sky!

Twirl and dance about the room.

Jenifer Edler
As You Grow Daycare
Trout Run, PA

Sing-Along Reminders

Lead youngsters in singing this friendly tune and they're sure to remember the important rule in each verse.

(sung to the tune of "The Wheels on the Bus")

The children in the room use [walking feet],
[Walking feet, walking feet].
The children in the room use [walking feet]
All through the day.

Continue with the following: *inside voices, friendly words*

Linda Cunningham
Vineland Elementary
Rotonda West, FL

Little Pumpkin

You'll see oodles of grins when youngsters perform this pumpkin-themed song!

(sung to the tune of "Five Little Ducks")

Green little pumpkin on the ground, *Make a small circle with fingers.*

Growing, growing orange and round. *Make a circle with arms.*

You'll be a jack-o'-lantern, big and bright, *Move arm circle above head.*

Just in time to light for Halloween night. *Move arm circle side to side.*

Halloween night, Halloween night, *Continue movement.*

Just in time to light for Halloween night. *Continue movement.*

LeeAnn Collins
Sunshine House Preschool
Lansing, MI

Mixed-Up Owls

Little ones will howl with delight at this adorable poem that helps develop phonological awareness!

Five baby owls learning to say *who*—
They flapped their wings and then said, "[Shoe]!"
Momma Owl wailed, "No! No! Not [shoe]!
Please, oh please, say, 'Who, who, who!'"

Continue with the following: *glue, blue, stew, moo, true, boo*

adapted from an idea by Nicole Furfaro
St. Paul Catholic School
Guelph, Ontario, Canada

Harvest Time

Youngsters thank farmers for their harvest with this catchy song! Lead youngsters in singing the entire song. Then repeat the second verse three more times, substituting a new food or foods for each repetition.

(sung to the tune of "London Bridge")

Farmers grow us many foods,
Many foods, many foods.
Farmers grow us many foods.
Thank you, farmers!

Farmers grow us [corn and squash],
[corn and squash], [corn and squash].
Farmers grow us [corn and squash].
Thank you, farmers!

Continue with the following: *pumpkins, potatoes, apples and yams*

Cherie Durbin
Hickory, NC

Diez Little Turkeys

Youngsters count in Spanish when they sing this terrific turkey tune!

(sung to the tune of "Ten Little Indians")

Uno little, *dos* little, *tres* little turkeys,
Cuatro little, *cinco* little, *seis* little turkeys,
Siete little, *ocho* little, *nueve* little turkeys.
Diez little turkeys on the farm!

Tonya Bays
Kinder Kampus Early Childhood Services
Corydon, IN

SONGS & SUCH

Snow Happy

Youngsters declare their happiness about snow with this catchy song! If it does not snow where you live, toss a handful of packing peanuts in your circle-time area so they resemble snow. Then lead students in singing the song. Repeat the song several times, changing the underlined action each time.

(sung to the tune of "If You're Happy and You Know It")

If you're happy that it snowed, [clap your hands].
If you're happy that it snowed, [clap your hands].
Oh, it's fluffy, and it's white—
Such a lovely, snowy sight!
If you're happy that it snowed, [clap your hands].

Sandra Rosen
Fascination Station
Latrobe, PA

Holiday Dreams

Have five youngsters lie on your floor and pretend to be asleep. Then lead students in singing the song, prompting one child to stand and then sit with the remaining students when indicated. Repeat the process for three more verses. Then sing the final verse with youngsters.

(sung to the tune of "Five Green and Speckled Frogs")

[Five] little girls and boys
Dreaming of lovely toys,
They know that Santa's on his way. (Ho! Ho!)
One child woke up and said,
"I will get out of bed!"
Now there are just [four] girls and boys. (Snore! Snore!)

Final verse:
One little girl or boy
Dreaming of lovely toys,
[He] knows that Santa's on his way. (Ho! Ho!)
That child woke up and said,
"I will get out of bed!"
Now there are zero girls and boys! (Hooray!)

adapted from an idea by Erin Cotter, MCD, Bayshore, NY

Colorful Stars

Attach a holiday tree cutout to a wall. Then make a supply of colorful star cutouts and give a star to each child. Hold up a star. Then lead students in reciting the rhyme, substituting the appropriate color. Next, have children with the corresponding stars stand and attach them to the tree. Repeat the rhyme with each remaining color.

We're looking for some stars for our holiday tree.
It's as lovely as can be!
Let's add [purple] stars, look and see—
Who has [purple] stars for our tree?

Melanie Mills
The Preschool of Whitehouse United Methodist Church
Whitehouse, NJ

Hanukkah Candles

Sing eight verses of this brilliant song—one for each day in the Hanukkah celebration!

(sung to the tune of "The Wheels on the Bus")

Let's light [one candle] for Hanukkah,
Hanukkah, Hanukkah.
Let's light [one candle] for Hanukkah
On day number [one].

LeeAnn Collins
Sunshine House Preschool
Lansing, MI

Five Little Penguins

Have youngsters stand to take part in this adorable action rhyme. Lead youngsters in reciting the rhyme five times, changing the number and holding up the corresponding number of fingers each time.

[Five] little penguin(s) standing in a row.   *Hold up [five] fingers.*
[Five] little penguin(s) standing in the snow.
Brrrr, it's cold! I cannot stay!   *Hug self and shiver.*
And one little penguin waddled away.   *Waddle in place.*

Mary Jean Sulham
Mount Carmel Head Start
Mount Carmel, PA

Martin's Wish

Commemorate Martin Luther King Day with several rounds of this simple song. If desired, give each child an instrument to play as he sings.

(sung to the tune of "Row, Row, Row Your Boat")

Martin had a dream
Of equality,
For yellow, red, black, and white
To live in harmony.

Marie E. Cecchini
West Dundee, IL

SONGS & SUCH

Making Valentines

Encourage youngsters to pantomime making a valentine with this fun action song! After youngsters sing the song, invite them to make valentines similar to those described.

(sung to the tune of "London Bridge")

Valentines are fun to make,
Fun to make, fun to make.
Valentines are fun to make.
Let's all make one!

First, we'll cut a paper heart,
Paper heart, paper heart.
First, we'll cut a paper heart.
Snip, snip, snip, snip!

Additional verses:
Next, we'll paint a silly face…. Brush, brush, brush, brush.
Now we'll glue on pretty lace…. Dab, dab, dab, dab.
We'll wait for our hearts to dry…. Ticktock, ticktock.
Then we'll hang them on the wall…. Aren't they lovely?

Cherie Durbin, Hickory, NC

Build a Rainbow

To make a prop for this song, draw a rainbow and cut out the separate arcs. Attach the hook side of a Velcro fastener to the back of each arc. Lead students in singing the first verse of the song. Then have a child attach the red arc to your flannelboard. Continue with each remaining verse, changing the color and ordinal number appropriately, until the entire rainbow is on the flannelboard.

(sung to the tune of "The Farmer in the Dell")

The [red] part goes up [first].
The [red] part goes up [first].
Heigh-ho, the rainbow.
The [red] part goes up [first].

Continue with the following: *orange, yellow, green, blue, violet*

Kelly Ash, Waukesha Head Start, Waukesha, WI

A Silly Song

Youngsters learn animal sounds with this grin-inducing sing-along! Lead youngsters in singing the song shown. Then ask the question below, encouraging students to respond accordingly as they point to their backs. Continue with the remaining verses, asking the question after each.

(sung to the tune of "If You're Happy and You Know It")

There's a [quack, quack] on my [back], on my [back].
There's a [quack, quack] on my [back], on my [back].
Yes, it's on my [back], you see.
What a silly place to be!
There's a [quack, quack] on my [back], on my [back].

Teacher: What's on my [back]?
Students: A [duck]!

Additional verses: *a moo, moo on my shoe; a neigh, neigh on my nose; a tweet, tweet on my tummy; a hee-haw on my head; a cluck, cluck on my chin*

Kathy Heiken, Kathy's Home Child Care, Clinton, IA

It's March!

Celebrate the month of March with this engaging action song!

(sung to the tune of "The Ants Go Marching")

Can you tell me what month it is?   *Throw arms out to side.*
It's March! It's March!   *March in place.*
Can you tell me what month it is?   *Throw arms out to side.*
It's March! It's March!   *March in place.*
Sometimes we sweat,   *Wipe forehead.*
And sometimes we freeze.   *Hug self and shiver.*
It snows and melts,   *Wiggle fingers like snowflakes.*
And there's quite a breeze.   *Wave arms gently in the air.*
And it blows us all around,   *Wave arms enthusiastically.*
And around, and around!
Whoosh, whoosh, whoosh!

Lisa Meeks, Fairview Early Education Center, Rockford, IL

SONGS & SUCH

Hopping Bunnies

Youngsters will jump for joy when they sing this sweet little song! Lead students in singing the first verse of the song loudly while they pantomime the actions. Continue leading youngsters in performing the remaining verses, prompting them to sing more quietly for each subsequent verse.

(sung to the tune of "When the Saints Go Marching In")

Oh, when the bunnies [come hopping in],
Oh, when the bunnies [come hopping in],
Oh, how I want to be in that garden
When the bunnies [come hopping in].

Continue with the following: *all nibble lunch, all go to sleep*

Karen Amatrudo, Madison, CT

Jelly Bean Jam

Here's a toe-tapping ode to jelly beans. If desired, give each child a small bottle partially filled with a few jelly beans (shaker). Then lead students in singing the song and shaking their instruments. Collect the instruments for safekeeping after the performance.

(sung to the tune of "Jingle Bells")

Jelly beans, jelly beans,
They aren't beans at all.
They are tasty candies
That are colorful and small.
Jelly beans, jelly beans,
They aren't beans at all.
They are tasty candies
That are colorful and small!

Sharon Vandike, Visitation School, Vienna, MO

Five Little Duckies

To make props for this song, attach five duckling cutouts (see page 163) to your board. Lead students in reciting the rhyme four times, pausing after each verse to have a youngster remove a duckling and answer the question.

(sung to the tune of "Five Little Ducks")

[Five] little ducks playing in a tub
Splish, splish, splash, and rub-a-dub-dub.
Mommy dried one and sent him away.
How many ducks were left to play?
Left to play, left to play,
How many ducks were left to play?

Cindy Kelley
St. Bernard School
Wabash, IN

Body Parts!

Have little ones perform this quick little chant, pointing to each body part when appropriate.

Elbow, elbow,	*Point to each elbow.*
Wrist, wrist.	*Point to each wrist.*
Fingers go like this, this.	*Wiggle fingers.*
Knees and toes,	*Touch knees; then touch toes.*
Hips and nose.	*Touch hips; then touch nose.*
That's the way it goes!	*Clap twice after the phrase.*

Denise Fisher
Orange United Methodist Preschool
Chapel Hill, NC

Cracker Chorus

Spotlight a tasty preschool favorite with this silly song! After leading students in performing the song, invite them to nibble on cheese and cracker sandwiches.

(sung to the tune of "My Bonnie Lies Over the Ocean")

I'm snacking on crackers—
    they're yummy.
I love them with my favorite spread!
They're munchy and crunchy and
    crumbly.
I make sandwiches without bread!

Crackers, crackers,
I eat them and brush off the crumbs,
    the crumbs!
Crackers, crackers,
I eat them and brush off the crumbs!

Rub tummy.

Pretend to apply spread from knife onto palm.
Move hands like mouths.

Stack hands one on top of the other.

Sway back and forth.
Brush off crumbs.

Sway back and forth.
Brush off crumbs.

Jacqueline Schiff
Moline, IL

Happy Mother's Day

Write the word *Mommy* on your board. Then lead students in singing the song six times, removing a letter and replacing it with a clap for each verse.

(sung to the tune of "Bingo")

I know someone who's very special.
Mommy is her name-o!
M-O-M-M-Y, M-O-M-M-Y, M-O-M-M-Y,
And Mommy is her name-o!

Karla Broad
Our Savior Preschool
Naples, FL

SONGS & SUCH

Let's Celebrate Summer!

Here's a catchy song just perfect for the summer season!

(sung to the tune of "This Old Man")

Summertime, it's such fun.
We play in the nice warm sun.
We can swim and splash and play out in the pool.
Summertime is really cool!

Deborah Garmon, Groton, CT

The Veggie Patch

Gather a basket and a variety of real or plastic vegetables. Lead students in singing the first verse of the song, inserting a child's name where indicated. Then invite the child to choose a vegetable, say its name, and place it in her basket. Lead students in singing the second verse of the song, inserting the appropriate vegetable name and pronoun.

(sung to the tune of "Pawpaw Patch")

Where, oh where, is dear little [Sarah]?
Where, oh where, is dear little [Sarah]?
Where, oh where, is dear little [Sarah]?
Way down yonder in the vegetable patch.

Picking [cucumbers] for [her] basket.
Picking [cucumbers] for [her] basket.
Picking [cucumbers] for [her] basket.
Way down yonder in the vegetable patch

Sandra Curtis, Browncroft Day Care Center, Rochester, NY

Picking Watermelon

You're sure to see oodles of grins when youngsters sing this song about a traditional summertime fruit!

(sung to the tune of "Clementine")

Picked a watermelon,
Picked a watermelon
That was growing in the sun.
So we sliced it,
And we ate it.
Then we picked another one!

Denise Dobbins, Elyria YMCA, Elyria, OH

Five Little Seashells

Attach five seashell cutouts to your board. Lead students in reciting the first couplet of the rhyme shown, encouraging them to enthusiastically wave their arms for the splash. Have a child remove a seashell. Repeat the process for the remaining verses.

Five little seashells lying on the shore.
Here comes a wave—SPLASH! Now there are four.

Four little seashells sitting by the sea.
Here comes a wave—SPLASH! Now there are three.

Three little seashells—that's just a few.
Here comes a wave—SPLASH! Now there are two.

Two little seashells basking in the sun.
Here comes a wave—SPLASH! That leaves one.

One little seashell and the day is done.
Here comes a wave—SPLASH! And now there are none.

Belinda Adkins, Jane Lew, WV

Wave Your Flag!

Spotlight the Fourth of July with this cute action poem!

Wave your flag for the Fourth of July.
Swing it proudly in the sky.
Stars and stripes in red, white, and blue

Decorate the flag for me and you!

Pretend to wave a flag.
Pretend to wave the flag higher.
Wiggle fingers for stars; move hand
* horizontally for stripes.*
Point to self and others.

LeeAnn Collins, Sunshine House Preschool, Lansing, MI

Picnic Time!

What are some picnic favorites? Youngsters list them in this entertaining chant!

Fried chicken, watermelon, apple pie.
Do you like picnics? So do I!
Hamburgers, ice cream, lemonade.
It's so hot—let's find some shade!
Potato salad, hot dogs taste so fine.
It's picnic, picnic, picnic time!

adapted from an idea by Heather Leverett

STORYTIME

Storytime

The Apple Pie Tree
Written by Zoe Hall
Illustrated by Shari Halpern

Two sisters delight in observing the seasonal changes of their cherished apple tree. Colorful collage illustrations and simple text depict how the tree changes from winter to fall and provides a tasty apple pie!

ideas contributed by Carole Watkins, Crown Point, IN

You bake the pie for ten hours!

Before You Read

This prereading activity is sure to inspire little ones to share their best apple pie recipe ideas! Show youngsters the cover of the book and then read aloud the title. Ask students whether they have ever helped make an apple pie. After a brief discussion, invite youngsters to describe how to make an apple pie; then record their recipe ideas on a sheet of chart paper. Finally, have little ones settle in for this enlightening read-aloud!

After You Read

Invite youngsters to make a delicious-looking apple pie—just like the one in the story! Give each child a brown construction paper copy of page 155. Encourage him to cut scraps of white construction paper so they resemble apple slices and then glue them to the dish. After he spreads a layer of glue over the apples, encourage him to sprinkle white glitter (sugar) and cinnamon over the apples. Now that looks and smells tasty!

Tasty Apple Pie!

Don't Let the Pigeon Drive the Bus!

Written and illustrated by Mo Willems

The bus driver in this story leaves his bus under the watchful eyes of the reader with one simple request—don't let the pigeon drive the bus! But the pigeon is determined to get its way.

ideas contributed by Carole Watkins, Crown Point, IN

I feel sad when Mommy says no.

Before You Read

Ask youngsters how they respond when they are told they cannot do something they want to do. For example, you might ask them if they feel sad, if they keep asking after being told no, or if they get angry and yell. After each child has had the opportunity to share, explain that the pigeon in the story you're about to read does all these things and more when it is told that it cannot drive a bus! Then have little ones settle in for this hilarious read-aloud.

After You Read

Review the events of the story with this entertaining song. If desired, invite a child to act out the part of the pigeon.

(sung to the tune of "The Wheels on the Bus")

The pigeon on the bus asks, "Can I drive, can I drive, can I drive?"
The pigeon on the bus asks, "Can I drive?" all through the town.

Continue with the following:
The children on the bus say, "No! No! No…"
The pigeon on the bus begs, "Please, please, please…"
The pigeon on the bus shouts, "That's not fair…"

Storytime

Harold and the Purple Crayon
Written and illustrated by Crockett Johnson

Harold decides to go for a moonlit walk, so he uses his purple crayon to draw a path and a moon to light the way. Soon his crayon is creating all sorts of adventures!

ideas contributed by Ada Goren, Winston-Salem, NC

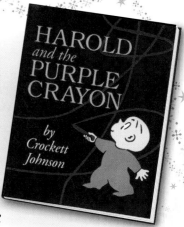

You should draw a cow!

Before You Read
Hold up a purple crayon and ask youngsters what you should draw. Take several suggestions and quickly draw the items on a sheet of chart paper. Next, hold up the cover of the book and explain that Harold has a purple crayon as well. Ask youngsters what they think he will draw. After they share their thoughts, have them settle in for this classic read-aloud.

After You Read
Attach a long sheet of white bulletin board paper to the floor. Give each child a purple crayon. Encourage youngsters to use their imaginations as they work together to create a class adventure. After each child has had the opportunity to contribute to the drawing, mount it to a wall and title it "Our Purple Crayon Adventure!"

Pumpkin Circle:
The Story of a Garden
Written by George Levenson
Photography by Shmuel Thaler

Clever, simple text and brilliant photos document the life cycle of a pumpkin from seed to pumpkin and back to the earth.

It's a pumpkin seed!

Before You Read

Display a pumpkin seed as you recite the poem shown. When the poem ends, encourage little ones to guess what type of seed it is about. After the seed has been correctly identified, read aloud this beautifully illustrated book.

Let's look at this seed before we read;
Then listen for some clues.
It comes from something fat and round
That grows on a vine along the ground.
Outside it has bright orange skin
That hides a gooey mess within!

After You Read

For each child, divide a paper plate into fourths. Then have her use the materials listed to decorate the plate to show the life cycle of a pumpkin.

Seed: seed cutout
Vine: leaf cutouts and green yarn
Flower: crumpled yellow tissue paper
Pumpkin: orange pumpkin cutout with a green paper stem

Storytime

Snowmen at Night
Written by Caralyn Buehner
Illustrated by Mark Buehner

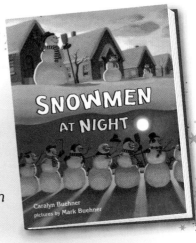

One wintry day, a young child builds a glorious snowman. But the following morning his snowman is droopy and disheveled—which leads him to imagine what snowmen do at night!

ideas contributed by Lucia Kemp Henry, Fallon, NV

They might play hide-and-seek!

Before You Read
This prereading activity is sure to inspire lots of creative thinking! Show youngsters the cover of the book and then read the title aloud. Ask students to imagine what types of things snowmen might do if they could move. Finally, have youngsters settle in for this rollicking tale of snowman adventures!

At night my snowman plays football!

After You Read
Invite each youngster to reveal his snowman's secret night-life with this art activity! Use a white crayon to program a class supply of black construction paper with the prompt "At night, my snowman…" Have each child sponge-paint a snowman on a sheet of programmed paper and decorate it as desired. Then read the prompt aloud and encourage him to dictate words for you to write to complete the sentence. If desired, bind the pages together to make a class book titled "Our Snowmen at Night."

Tacky the Penguin
Written by Helen Lester
Illustrated by Lynn Munsinger

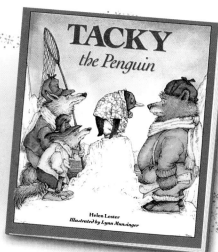

Tacky is an odd, unconventional penguin with a group of very dignified friends. Although his outlandish behaviors annoy his companions, they come in handy when his penguin pals are in need of rescue!

ideas contributed by Lucia Kemp Henry, Fallon, NV

> I think Tacky gets messy when he eats!

Before You Read
After reading the title aloud, ask youngsters to look at Tacky's picture and describe what his personality might be like based on the picture. Open the book to the first double-page spread that shows Tacky and his companions. After students view all the penguins, ask each child whether he thinks Tacky might act differently than his posh pals; then have him explain his response. Finally, read the story aloud to see whether youngsters' first impressions of Tacky and his friends were true!

(sung to the tune of "Row, Row, Row Your Boat")

We're the penguin pals, such a pretty sight.
We are lovely, neat and good, quiet and polite.

Now we're silly birds, crazy and so loud.
You might say we're tacky, but we are smart and proud!

After You Read
Celebrate the penguins' differences by inviting youngsters to act like Tacky and his nearly perfect peers. Encourage little ones to march like Tacky's companions and then like Tacky. Next, have them pretend to dive elegantly like Tacky's friends and then splash like Tacky. To conclude the activity, lead students in singing the first verse of the song shown in a calm, sophisticated style and the remaining verse in a wacky Tacky manner!

Storytime

Where Is the Green Sheep?
Written by Mem Fox
Illustrated by Judy Horacek

*Clever art and simple text are sure to engage
youngsters in the quest to find a missing sheep. But where can it be?*

ideas contributed by Ada Goren, Winston-Salem, NC

I found the sheep!

Before You Read
Hide a toy sheep or a sheep cutout (see page 96) in your classroom. Show the cover of the book and read the title aloud. Then say, "I don't know where the green sheep is, but I have a sheep right here." Reach for the sheep and then exclaim with great dramatic flair that it's missing! Invite little ones to help you find the sheep; then settle in for this entertaining read-aloud.

After You Read
To make this class book, give each child a copy of page 156. Invite her to glue a construction paper cloud shape to the sheet; then have her decorate the shape so it resembles a sheep from the book. Next, have her name the color of her sheep and where her sheep might be. Write the information in the spaces provided. Bind the finished pages together between two covers and title the book "Where Are Our Sheep?"

Where is the __pink__ sheep?

It is __at the store__

150

The Foot Book

Written and illustrated by Dr. Seuss

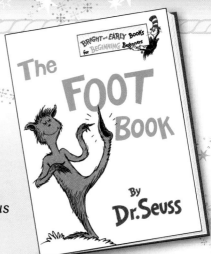

Oh, there are so many feet your little ones will meet in this delightful Dr. Seuss classic! Humorous illustrations and whimsical rhymes about feet highlight the wonderful world of opposites.

My feet!

Before You Read

Introduce Dr. Seuss's wacky book of opposites by reciting the rhyme shown. Once little ones have correctly guessed that the book's subject is feet, invite youngsters to join you for this classic read-aloud.

We're going to read a book today
About some body parts.
They're down below your eyes and chin;
They're down below your heart.
They're farther down, below your hips;
And down below your knees.
They're the parts you walk on.
Can you name them for me, please?

Big feet and small feet,
Fast and slow feet too.
Can you guess whose
feet these are?
Do they belong to you?

After You Read

Have each child attach a photo of himself to a sheet of construction paper. Then help him attach to the photo a paper flap programmed with the poem shown, making sure that only his feet show below the flap. To play this guessing game, hold up one of the projects and read the poem aloud. Then have youngsters try to guess the identity of the child. After several guesses, lift the flap to reveal the youngster's face.

Cindy Hubbard
Bunche Early Childhood Development Center
Tulsa, OK

Storytime

Muncha! Muncha! Muncha!
Written by Candace Fleming
Illustrated by G. Brian Karas

When the sun goes down and the moon comes up, three hungry bunnies fill their tummies with vegetables from Mr. McGreely's garden. As hard as he tries to protect his veggies, the motivated munchers always outsmart him!

ideas contributed by Lucia Kemp Henry, Fallon, NV

I think the rabbits eat all the carrots!

Before You Read
Conceal in a sack several vegetables, a garden trowel, a watering can, and three rabbit cutouts (see page 17). In turn, remove each item from the bag (leaving the rabbits for last) and place it on a sheet of brown paper. Lead youngsters to guess that the story is about a vegetable garden. Then reveal the rabbit cutouts and have students predict what they think happens in the story. Finally, read the story aloud and have little ones see whether their predictions came true.

After You Read
Place a class supply of carrot cutouts in the center of your circle. Invite three students to pretend to be rabbits. Turn your back to the group and slowly chant, "Tippy, tippy, tippy, pat! Muncha! Muncha! Muncha!" While your back is turned, each rabbit takes a carrot to her seat. When you finish the chant and turn around, notice the carrots missing from your garden and react with great dramatic flair! Continue in the same way until all the carrots are gone. Then have your little rabbits pretend to munch on their carrots.

Duck on a Bike

Written and illustrated by David Shannon

When an adventurous duck takes a spin on a bike, his actions spur an array of thoughts among his barnyard companions. But after each critic gives it a try, they all think it's a great idea!

A duck waddles and says, "Quack, quack!"

Before You Read

Before revealing the cover of the book, invite youngsters to name things a duck might do, such as swim, fly, quack, sleep, eat, lay eggs, and waddle. After youngsters reveal their thoughts, display the cover of the book and read the title aloud. Ask little ones whether they think the book will describe a true story or one that is pretend; then have them explain their answers. Finally, read this delightful tale aloud.

I saw <u>a monkey</u> riding a bike. It rode to the store and bought some bananas.

by <u>Kyle</u>

After You Read

Give each child a copy of page 157. Read the prompt aloud and encourage the student to name an animal of his choice. Then have him tell something about the animal's bike-riding adventure, such as where the animal was going or something that happened along the way. Record his dictation; then have him illustrate the page. If desired, bind the pages together to make a class book titled "Animals on Bikes."

Storytime

Caps for Sale
Written and illustrated by Esphyr Slobodkina

In this classic tale, a weary cap peddler stops to enjoy an afternoon nap under a big tree. But when he awakens, he is shocked to find that a band of mischievous monkeys has taken all his caps!

ideas contributed by Ada Goren, Winston-Salem, NC

Before You Read

This prereading idea is sure to raise a few eyebrows and induce lots of giggles! Gather several hats and conceal all but one in a bag. Don that hat as you sit down for storytime. Then, in turn, remove each hat from the bag and stack it atop your head. After the giggling subsides, explain that today's story is about a man who sells caps that he stacks upon his head. Then invite little ones to settle in for this entertaining read-aloud.

After You Read

Here's a fun way to retell the story. Have each child attach a cap cutout (pattern on page 158) to a headband. Then size the band to the child's head. Pretend to be the peddler by affixing a paper mustache to your upper lip. Invite each child (monkey) to wear his cap. Then reenact the story by imitating the peddler's actions and saying, "You monkeys, you! You give me back my caps!" Encourage each of your little monkeys to respond by imitating the monkeys' actions and saying, "Tsz, tsz, tsz."

Tsz, tsz, tsz.

Tasty Apple Pie!

Where is the _____ sheep?

It is _____

Note to the teacher: Use with "After You Read" on page 150.

I saw _____
riding a bike. It

by _____

Cap Pattern

Use with "After You Read" on page 154.

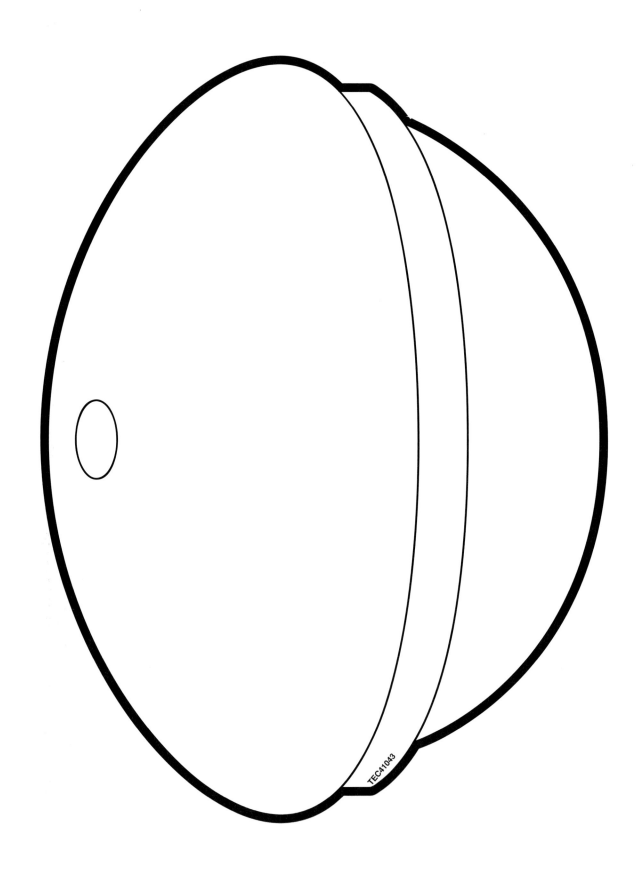

TEC41043

BOOK UNITS

Books With Predictable Text

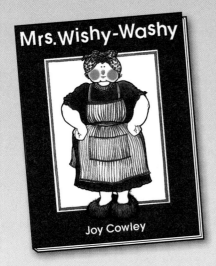

Mrs. Wishy-Washy

Joy Cowley

ideas contributed by Ada Goren, Winston-Salem, NC

Mrs. Wishy-Washy
Written by Joy Cowley
Illustrated by Elizabeth Fuller

What happens when a duck, a cow, and a pig get into mischief and play in mud puddles? Why, they get a good scrubbing from Mrs. Wishy-Washy, of course. But those animals won't stay clean for long!

What Will She Wash?

Building prior knowledge

Before reading the book, show youngsters the book cover and read aloud the title. Then ask, "What can you tell me about Mrs. Wishy-Washy?" Lead youngsters to conclude that she is dressed to do some washing. Then ask each child to suggest what she might wash. Finally, share the story of this scrub-happy lady and her muddy farm pals!

Mud Masterpiece

Developing fine-motor skills

These muddy farm animals are a mess—just like the animals in the story! Invite each youngster to dip a plastic farm animal toy into a shallow pan of brown paint (mud). Then encourage her to move the animal across a sheet of paper. Have her repeat the process with other plastic farm animals.

Animal Cleanup

Recreating an event from a story

Squirt scented dish soap in your water table. Then place plastic farm animals and fingernail brushes nearby. A youngster places a farm animal in the water and then scrubs him while saying, "Wishy-washy, wishy-washy," just like in the story. Encourage youngsters to get each animal squeaky clean.

Brown Bear, Brown Bear, What Do You See?

Written by Bill Martin Jr.
Illustrated by Eric Carle

Mix colorful critters with a catchy chant that youngsters can master in no time, and you'll have this story—a true preschool classic!

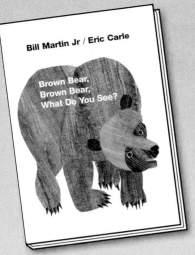

What Do You See?

Speaking

Youngsters review the colors and animals in the book with this simple activity! Open the book to show one of the colorful illustrations. Then ask a youngster, "[Cody, Cody], what do you see?" Encourage him to reply, "I see a [red bird] looking at me." Continue in the same way for each remaining youngster, varying the pictures shown.

Brown Bear Sees Students!

Familiarizing youngsters with spelling their first names
Have each child color a bear cutout (see the pattern on page 163) and attach it to a sheet of construction paper. Have each youngster attach a photo of himself to the sheet as well. Give each child letter cards that correspond to the letters in his name. Help the child arrange the cards on the construction paper to spell his name and then have him glue them in place. Mount these projects with the title "Brown Bear, Brown Bear, Who Do You See?"

Jayne E. Jaskolski, Twenty-First Street School, Milwaukee, WI

Book Review

Developing recall skills

Make a paper chain with colorful strips that correspond to the colors in the story. Then hold up the paper chain and touch the brown link. Have students chant, "Brown Bear, brown bear, what do you see?" Touch the red link and prompt students to say, "I see a red bird looking at me!" Continue in the same way with the remaining links.

Joyce Cooper, Pittman Elementary, Springfield, MO

Have You Seen My Duckling?

Written and illustrated by Nancy Tafuri

A mother duck takes her ducklings out for a swim, but when one duckling separates from the group, Mother Duck spends the day asking her pond friends if they've seen her wayward child.

Quack and Waddle

Building excitement for a story

Before reading the story, explain that the storytime selection for the day will feature a mother duck and her ducklings. Pretend to be a mother duck and lead your students (ducklings) around the room, having them quack and flap their arms as if their arms were wings. Finally, have them settle down for a read-aloud of this delightful book.

Who Has It?

Following rules to play a game

Have students sit in a circle. Then have one child cover his eyes while you have a second youngster sit on a duckling cutout (see the pattern on page 163). Instruct the child to open his eyes and then go to one of his classmates and ask, "Have you seen my duckling?" If the child does not have the cutout, she says no and the youngster moves on to a different child. If she is concealing the cutout, she says yes and reveals the cutout.

There's That Duckling!

Developing fine-motor skills

Youngsters make this easy artwork to spotlight the wandering duckling! Have each child cut or tear strips of green construction paper. Encourage her to glue the strips to a sheet of blue construction paper so they resemble the water plants in the story. Next, have her glue a yellow duckling cutout (see page 163) to her pond. If desired, encourage the child to add a butterfly sticker to her paper—just like the butterfly in the story!

Bear Pattern
Use with "Brown Bear Sees Students!" on page 161.

TEC41038

Duckling Pattern
Use with "Who Has It?" and "There's That Duckling!" on page 162.

TEC41038

Families

Written and photo-illustrated by Ann Morris
Families work, eat, and play together in this nonfiction book. Simple, straightforward text accompanies engaging photographs that highlight ways families can be alike and different.

ideas by Ada Goren, Winston-Salem, NC

Teachers Have Families Too!
Building excitement for the read-aloud
Pique youngsters' interest in the read-aloud by showing them a photograph of your own family! Display a photograph of your family. Then point to each family member and explain his or her relationship to you. Next, tell students that the book you're about to read shows more photographs of families, and the families come from different countries throughout the world. Then settle youngsters in for this interesting read-aloud.

Caretakers
Speaking to answer a question
Ann Morris points out that children live with different types of caretakers, such as parents, grandparents, foster parents, and adoptive parents. Invite youngsters to tell who takes care of them with this simple activity! Lead students in singing the song shown. Then have a volunteer share the names of the people who take care of him. Continue in the same way, repeating the song and then asking another child about his caretakers.

(sung to the tune of "Row, Row, Row Your Boat")

Who do you live with?
Who takes care of you?
Tell us about your family.
Who takes care of you?

I help my mom put away the spoons and forks!

Helping Hands
Speaking to share information
Revisit the book and have youngsters identify photographs that show members of a family helping each other. Explain that the phrase "give a helping hand" means to help someone with her work. Give a volunteer a hand cutout and ask him how he gives a helping hand to his family. After he is finished sharing, encourage him to give the hand to a classmate. Continue in the same way until each youngster has an opportunity to share.

Let's Compare!
Identifying similarities and differences among people
Have students compare photographs of families from the book with this small-group activity. Choose two facing pages in the book that show photographs of two families. Have preschoolers study the photos. Then encourage them to name ways the families are the same. After several minutes of discussion, prompt them to share ways the families appear to be different.

Tasty Meals
Appreciating similarities and differences among people
Gather a small group of youngsters. Then help students point out photographs in the story that show people preparing or eating food. Give each child a paper plate. Then encourage her to draw on the plate a picture of a food her family likes to eat. Have her identify the food as you write her words below the picture.

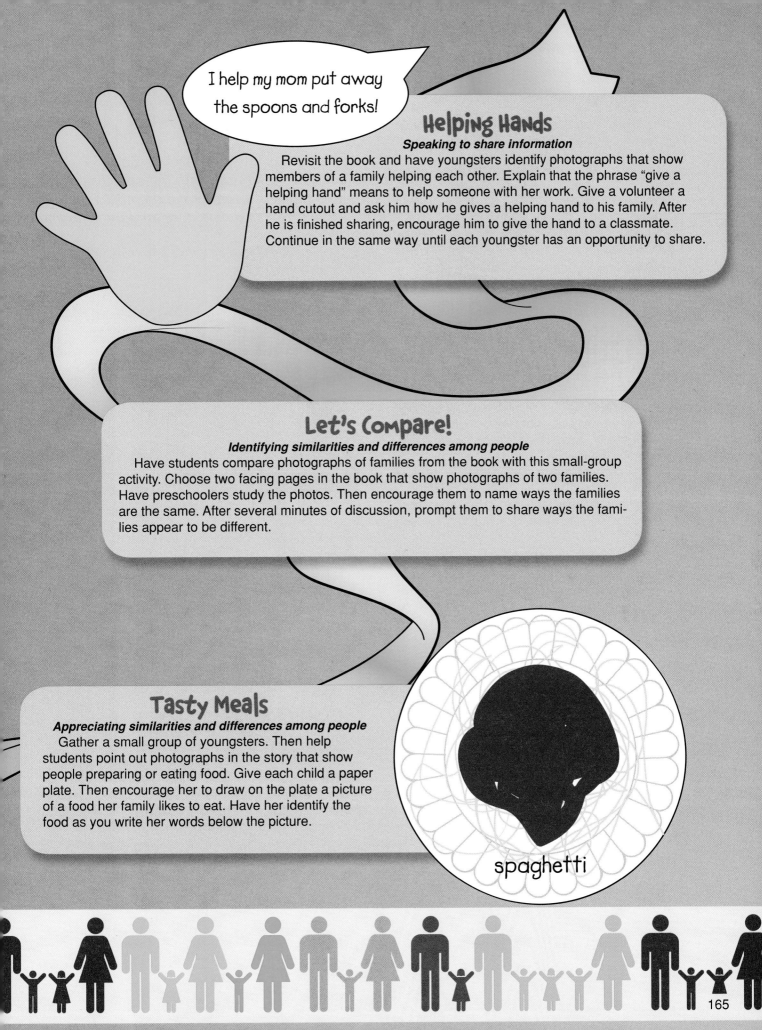

spaghetti

Snowballs

Written and illustrated by Lois Ehlert
Combine a sack of "good stuff" with the perfect snowball day and what do you get? An entire snow family! The unique collage illustrations in this simple story are sure to fascinate your youngsters!

ideas contributed by Carole J. Watkins, Crown Point, IN

Really Good Stuff

Promoting interest in a story

Invite youngsters to ponder a selection of good stuff with this prereading activity. Display a winter hat, a piece of popcorn, several kernels of corn, two raisins, a strawberry, and a bird cutout. Then ask, "What do you think these items could be used for?" After youngsters have shared their ideas, reveal the cover of the book and explain that the same items are used to decorate the snow dad in the story. Then have youngsters settle in for a read-aloud of this vibrantly illustrated book.

Snow Creations

Responding to the book through art

At this center, youngsters use items to create snowpals reminiscent of those in the story. Place white play dough at a table along with a variety of items such as fabric scraps, craft feathers, tinted pasta, ribbon, twigs, pipe cleaners, and any other collectibles that will inspire youngsters' creativity. Encourage each child to visit the center and mold the play dough into a snow character. Then have him decorate it as desired.

Flock of Birds

Estimating

During a rereading of the story, have students focus on the birds scattered throughout the pages of the book. Next, ask each child to guess how many birds are in the story. Record student responses on chart paper. Then lead youngsters in counting the birds aloud as you review the pages of the book with the class. Finally, compare the actual number of birds to student guesses.

How many 🐦 ?	
Kira	7
Matthew	10
Miguel	5
Jennifer	12
Zachary	9
Marta	4

On a perfect snowball day, I will build a snow ballerina!

Perfect Snowball Day

Dictating words to complete a sentence

Give each child a copy of page 168. Invite her to cut pictures of items from magazines to dress her own special snow character. Have her glue the cutouts to the page. Then read the prompt aloud and encourage her to dictate words to complete the sentence.

Snow Dad Came to School

Dramatizing a song

Here's a fun way to revisit the snow characters in the story! Have little ones sit in your large-group area. Invite a volunteer (snow dad) to stand. Lead students in singing the first verse of the song while the snow dad walks around the group. Prompt the snow dad to choose a snow mom. Then have them clasp hands and walk around the group as youngsters sing the second verse. Continue playing the game. Then, during the final verse, prompt the seated students to stand and hold their arms to resemble sun rays as the snow characters melt slowly to the floor.

(sung to the tune of "The Farmer in the Dell")

The snow dad came to school,
The snow dad came to school.
Heigh-ho, a snowy day!
The snow dad came to school.

Continue with the following:
The snow dad picks a mom.
The snow mom picks a boy.
The snow boy picks a girl.
The snow girl picks a baby.
The snow baby picks a cat.
The snow cat picks a dog.
The snow dog picks a sun.
The sun will make us melt.

On a perfect snowball day, I will build

Note to the teacher: Use with "Perfect Snowball Day" on page 167.

A Color of His Own

Written and illustrated by Leo Lionni

A chameleon desperately wants to have a color like all the other animals. In his search for one color he finds something even better—a friend who changes colors just like him.

ideas contributed by Lucia Kemp Henry, Fallon, NV

Leo Lionni
A Color of His Own

My Own Color
Making a personal connection
Before reading the story, show little ones the cover of the book and read the title aloud. Then invite each child to name a color of his own that he likes to wear, color pictures with, or have around him. Explain that a chameleon changes colors all the time and doesn't have a color of his own. Ask students how this would make them feel. After youngsters share their thoughts, have students settle in for a read-aloud of the story.

Leaves for Chameleons
Identifying and matching colors
The chameleon in the story changes colors to match the leaves he sits on. Youngsters will notice that the chameleons in this activity match their leaves as well! Place in a bag a class supply of colorful chameleon cutouts (pattern on page 171). Then prepare large leaf cutouts in matching colors. Place the leaves on the floor and have little ones sit in a circle around them. Have a youngster remove a chameleon from the bag and name its color. Then direct her to place it on the correct leaf. Continue until each child has a turn.

Hide-and-Seek

Writing

When the chameleon sits on a lemon, he is yellow; and when he sits on a leaf, he is green. With this activity, your little ones choose something the chameleon could sit on and what his color would be. Have each child draw an object on a sheet of paper. Then give her a chameleon cutout (see page 171). Have her put the chameleon above the object, color him to match, and then glue him in place. Finally, have her dictate words to add to her page.

When the chameleon is on an apple, he is red.

Anna

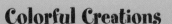

Pretty Patterns

Matching

To prepare for this activity, make copies of page 171 on animal-print scrapbook paper. Then cut out the patterns. Revisit the part of the story where the chameleon is striped like the tiger. Then give each student a chameleon. Direct each student to find a partner with a matching chameleon and have the pair sit together in a designated area. Invite each pair to hold up their chameleons and name an animal that has a similar appearance.

Colorful Creations

Responding to the book through art

Use the delightful illustrations of this book to inspire your little artists. Invite each student to use a favorite color of fingerpaint to paint a sheet of paper. Have her place a chameleon cutout (see page 171) on the wet paint. Then have her fingerpaint over the chameleon. Finally, encourage her to sprinkle glitter in the same color over the project. Display the artwork on a board titled "Where Are the Chameleons?"

Chameleon Patterns

Use with "Leaves for Chameleons" on page 169 and "Hide-and-Seek," "Pretty Patterns," and "Colorful Creations" on page 170.

TEC41043

TEC41043

Harry the Dirty Dog

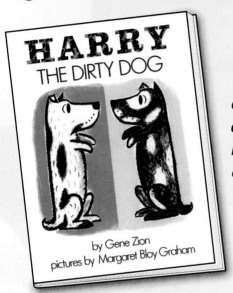

Written by Gene Zion
Illustrated by Margaret Bloy Graham

Harry the dog doesn't like bath time! So one day he buries the scrub brush and plays outside all day. Harry becomes so dirty his family doesn't recognize him. Perhaps it's time for Harry to clean up his act—at least for a little while.

ideas contributed by Tricia Brown, Bowling Green, KY

Bath Time Bubbles

Developing interest in the story

Gather a bottle of bubbles and a bubble wand and then blow bubbles throughout the classroom. Tell students the bubbles remind you of bath time. Invite volunteers to recount experiences they've had getting really dirty and needing a bath. Then explain that the storytime selection is about a dog who doesn't like to take baths at all. Finally, read aloud this classic story.

Where's Harry?

Dramatizing a story

Youngsters revisit the story with dramatic play! Stock a center with a stuffed dog, a towel, a plastic bucket, a brush, and an empty shampoo bottle. One student secretly hides the dog for other students to find. Once the dog is found, all the students at the center pretend to give it a bath.

They should use a washcloth with frogs on it.
Sarah

Harry should have more bath toys.
Ian

The people could add lots of bubbles.
Charlie

Fun in the Tub
Critical thinking

Harry's family needs some bath-time advice. Give each student a construction paper copy of page 174 and invite him to paint the bubble using pink and blue watercolors. When the paint is dry, help him cut out the bubble. Then ask him how to make bath time more fun for Harry and use a marker to write his words on the bubble. Mount the finished projects on a wall above a large tub cutout.

Clean or Dirty
Developing fine-motor skills

Youngsters revisit dirty Harry and clean Harry with this project and display. Divide a bulletin board or section of wall space in half. Then label one half *Clean* and the remaining half *Dirty*. Give each child a copy of the dog patterns on page 175. Have her make a few black fingerprints on one dog and many fingerprints on the remaining dog. Then help her cut out the dogs and attach them to the board.

Clean or Dirty?

Harry's Adventure
Retelling a story, participating in a song

To help little ones recount Harry's day, lead them in singing the featured song. After students are familiar with the lyrics, invite them to add motions.

(sung to the tune of "London Bridge")

1. Dirty Harry needs a bath,
   Needs a bath, needs a bath.
   Dirty Harry needs a bath.
   Where's the scrub brush?

2. Dirty Harry runs away,
   Runs away, runs away.
   Dirty Harry runs away.
   Where is Harry?

3. Dirty Harry wants a hug,
   Wants a hug, wants a hug.
   Dirty Harry wants a hug.
   He's too dirty.

4. Dirty Harry finds his brush,
   Finds his brush, finds his brush.
   Dirty Harry finds his brush.
   It is bath time!

Bubble Pattern
Use with "Fun in the Tub" on page 173.

TEC41042

TEC41042

TEC41042

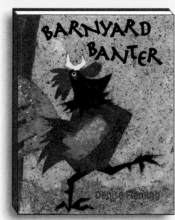

Barnyard Banter

There are a variety of noisy animals in this barnyard. But where is Goose? Goose is busy chasing a butterfly!

Where Is Goose?
Using positional words

The narrator repeatedly asks, "Where is Goose?" No doubt youngsters will be fascinated to find out there are several geese right in their school! Cut out copies of the goose pattern on page 179 and place them around your school. Then take youngsters on a walk, encouraging them to notice things around them. Whenever you are near a goose, prompt students to ask, "Where is Goose?" Then have youngsters find the goose and describe its location using positional words, such as, "Goose is beside the exit sign!"

Janice Wiginton, Treasure Patch Kids Preschool, Round Rock, TX

Denise Fleming Books

ideas contributed by Lucia Kemp Henry, Fallon, NV

Down on the Farm
Classifying

Before this engaging read-aloud, show students the cover of the book and ask them where they think it takes place. When they guess that the story takes place on a farm, ask them whether they think there will be a tiger in the story and lead them to conclude that it would be silly for a tiger to show up on a farm. Continue suggesting other animal character options, both silly and appropriate. Then have students settle in for this read-aloud.

Boisterous Barnyard!
Recalling story details

There are many noisy animals in this story! Prompt little ones to recall the animals in the story and the noises they make; write each animal name and noise on a sheet of chart paper. Have a child choose an animal. Then lead students in reciting the rhyme shown, inserting the animal's name and noise. Repeat the process for the remaining animals.

Barnyard banter—make some noise!
We're not really girls and boys.
We are [cows]!
[Moo! Moo! Moo!]

Mystery Box
Building interest in the story

The mysterious box in the book grabs Buster's attention. You can grab youngsters' attention in a similar way! Place the book and a stuffed kitten in a lidded box. Have students predict what might be in the box. Then open the box and remove the stuffed animal. Introduce her as Betty and explain that Betty shows up in the story in a big box just like the box in the classroom. Then take out the book and read the story aloud.

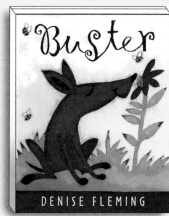

Buster

When a kitten comes along and invades Buster's personal space, Buster runs away to a place that's feline free. But he soon discovers that there is no place like home and that the kitten is a fine companion.

A Wonderful Review
Speaking to give an opinion

On the back of the book, Denise Fleming has added simple book reviews from some four-legged friends. Read the reviews aloud. If possible, share an online review of the story too. Next, ask youngsters to share their own reviews of the story. Write each review on a sticky note and attach it to the back cover of the book.

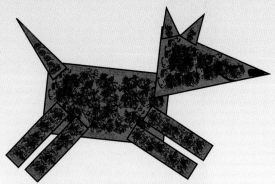

A Buster Craft
Developing fine-motor skills

For each child, cut shapes from brown construction paper to make the craft shown. Have students study a picture of Buster from the story. Discuss the colors Denise Fleming has included in her character. Next, have students glue the shapes together, as shown, to create Buster. Then have them sponge-paint Buster a reddish brown color. When the paint is dry, prompt them to add details such as facial features and blue edging.

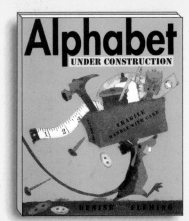

Alphabet Under Construction

Mouse uses his many skills to construct all the letters in the alphabet!

button
erase
fold
glue
hang
measure
nail
roll
unroll
vacuum
zip

So Many Skills
Making a personal connection

Before reading the story, display a chart with the words shown. Tell students that the book you're about to read is about a mouse who can do all the skills on the list. Read the list aloud. Then have students share their experiences with the skills, prompting them to identify what they can do with each skill. Finally, have students listen to a read-aloud of this creative story!

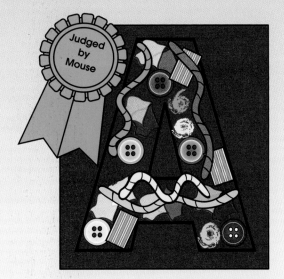

Letter Toolbox
Matching letters

With this activity, youngsters find letter cards to match the letters in the story. In advance, place letter cards on a tabletop and set a toolbox nearby. As you reread the story aloud, have students find each appropriate letter card and place it in the toolbox.

Crafty Construction
Responding to a story through art

With this center, little ones can be creative just like Mouse! Place letter outlines at a center. Provide a variety of construction items, such as jumbo buttons, scrapbook paper, wallpaper scraps, yarn, tissue paper, chalk, glue, and lunch bag pieces. Invite each youngster to use these items and a letter outline to construct his own unique letter. Then post the letters in your classroom and attach a blue ribbon (see page 180) to each one.

TEC41041

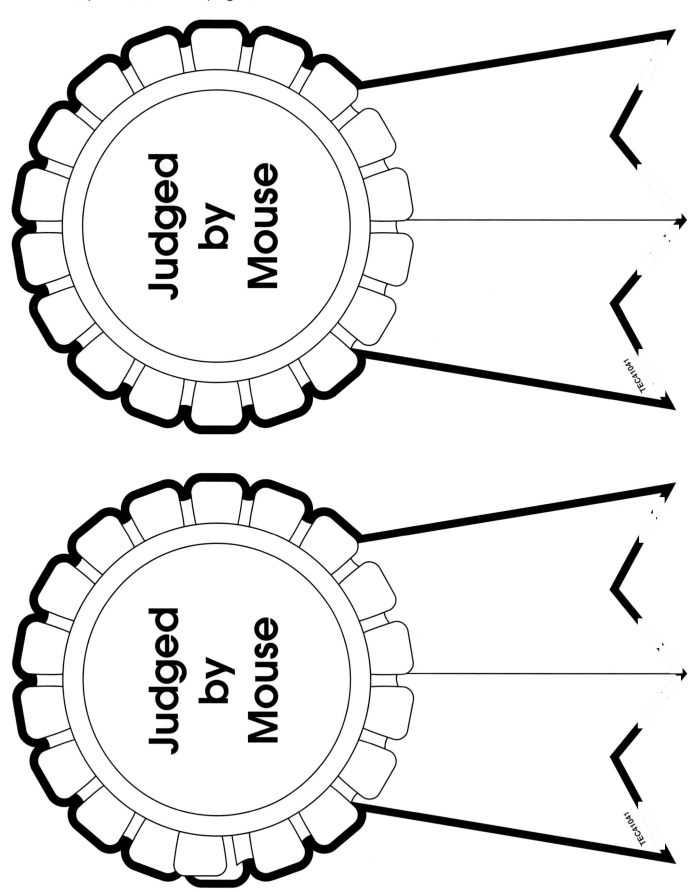

Judged
by
Mouse

Judged
by
Mouse

TEC41041

TEC41041

CENTER UNITS

Colorful Centers

These vivid centers focus on a variety of colors!

ideas contributed by Lucia Kemp Henry, Fallon, NV

Green, Green Grass
Sensory Center

To prepare, place green paper shreds in your sensory table. Gather pairs of green items and tuck one item from each pair into the paper shreds. Attach the remaining items to a sheet of tagboard and place it near the table. A child visits the center, removes an item from the table, and then places it next to the matching item on the tagboard. He continues in the same way with each remaining item.

Sunshine Snip
Fine-Motor Area

Trace triangles on separate scraps of yellow construction paper. Then place the triangles at a center along with scissors, glue sticks, and a large yellow circle cutout labeled with a smiling face (sun). Youngsters visit the center, cut out triangles, and glue them around the sun so they resemble rays.

Orange Impressions

Play Dough Center

Students make an "a-peeling" impression with this fun idea! Place orange play dough at a center along with several unpeeled oranges. A visiting child flattens a ball of play dough. Then he gently presses and rolls oranges over the play dough, leaving unique orange skin impressions in the dough.

Beautiful Blue Sky

Art Center

To prepare, gather tissue paper in different shades of blue and cut the tissue paper into squares. Place at a table the squares, slightly diluted glue, a paintbrush, white construction paper, and bluebird cutouts. A youngster brushes glue over a portion of his paper and then presses tissue paper squares over the glue. He continues until the entire paper is covered with tissue paper. Then he glues a bluebird in the middle of his beautiful blue sky.

Bunches of Grapes

Math Center

Youngsters practice one-to-one correspondence with this yummy-looking activity! In advance, draw bunches of grapes on separate paper plates. Place the plates at a center along with a supply of purple pom-poms. A child visits the center and chooses a plate. Then she places a pom-pom on each grape. She continues in the same manner with the remaining plates.

Rainbow Arcs
Flannelboard Center
Little ones practice seriation while creating a beautiful rainbow! Draw and color a rainbow on a sheet of construction paper. Then cut apart the rainbow's arcs. To ready the arcs for flannelboard use, attach the loop side of a Velcro fastener to each one. Place a flannelboard at a center with the arcs nearby. A visiting child places each arc on the board in size order. Then he identifies each color. Now that's one gorgeous rainbow!

Puzzle Pairs
Literacy Center
Write color words on coordinating craft foam strips. Then puzzle-cut each strip and place the puzzles at a center. A child chooses a puzzle piece and then finds its match. He puts the puzzle together and then runs his finger beneath the word as he says the color name.

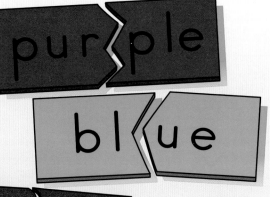

Songbook of Colors
Writing Center
Little ones will enjoy singing about their favorite color with this class book idea! Give each child a copy of page 185. Help her write her name and her favorite color on the appropriate lines. Next, have her choose an item in her favorite color from a magazine or grocery store circular. Encourage her to cut out the picture and glue it to the bottom of the page and then color the border to match. Then bind the finished pages together between two covers and title the book "Our Favorite Colors." At circle time, lead youngsters in singing aloud each page of this colorful class-made book!

adapted from an idea by Kristen Hanson
Mayville State University Child Development Programs
Mayville, ND

Our Favorite Colors
(sung to the tune of "Mary Had a Little Lamb")
Hannah has a favorite color,
Favorite color, favorite color.
Hannah has a favorite color
And yellow is its name.

Our Favorite Colors

(sung to the tune of "Mary Had a Little Lamb")

_____ has a favorite color,

Favorite color, favorite color.

_____ has a favorite color

And _____ is its name.

Note to the teacher: Use with "Songbook of Colors" on page 184.

185

Peppermint Centers

Puffy Candy Canes

Math Center

Youngsters practice copying a pattern when they create these cute candy canes! In advance, decorate a candy cane cutout (pattern on page 188) with red and white pom-poms in an *AB* pattern as shown. Place the sample at a table along with a class supply of candy cane cutouts, red and white pom-poms, and glue. A child visits the center and glues pom-poms to a candy cane in an *AB* pattern, using the sample as a guide.

Joy Barrett
Park Center Preschool
Glenview, IL

Sound Stocking

Literacy Center

A candy cane is more than just candy with this fun idea! Cut apart a copy of the picture cards from page 189 and place them in a stocking. Give each student a candy cane. Have youngsters hold the candy canes upside down so they resemble the letter *J*; then have each child make the letter sound. Next, prompt a child to remove a card from the stocking. If the pictured object begins with the /j/ sound, youngsters hold their candy canes upside down. If not, the candy canes are held in an upright position.

Sue Fleischmann
Catholic East Elementary
Milwaukee, WI

Twisty Canes
Fine-Motor Area

For each student, twist together a red and a white pipe cleaner at one end. Then place the pipe cleaners at a center. A child twists a pipe cleaner set together until he reaches the opposite end. Then he bends the top so it resembles a candy cane. For an added challenge, students twist together red, white, and green pipe cleaners!

Karla Broad, Our Savior Preschool
Naples, FL

A Sweet Heart
Writing Center

This card delivers a heartfelt message! Provide construction paper cards, candy canes, copies of the poem below, and a photo of each child's face. A child glues a copy of the poem to the inside of the card. Next to the poem, she draws a picture of herself with the intended recipient and then writes her name. Finally, she glues her photo to the front. Then she glues the candy canes to the card to make a heart shape.

Two striped candy canes,
As simple as can be,
Together make a heart
That sends love to you from me!

adapted from an idea by Sue Fleischmann
Catholic East Elementary
Milwaukee, WI

Positively Peppermint!
Sensory Center

To prepare, fill your sensory table with paper shreds. Hide an assortment of small wrapped candy canes and miniature mint chocolate candies among the shreds. Attach a piece of each type of candy to a separate container. A youngster searches for the candy and sorts the pieces she finds into the containers. When she leaves the center, she takes a piece of candy with her for a special treat!

187

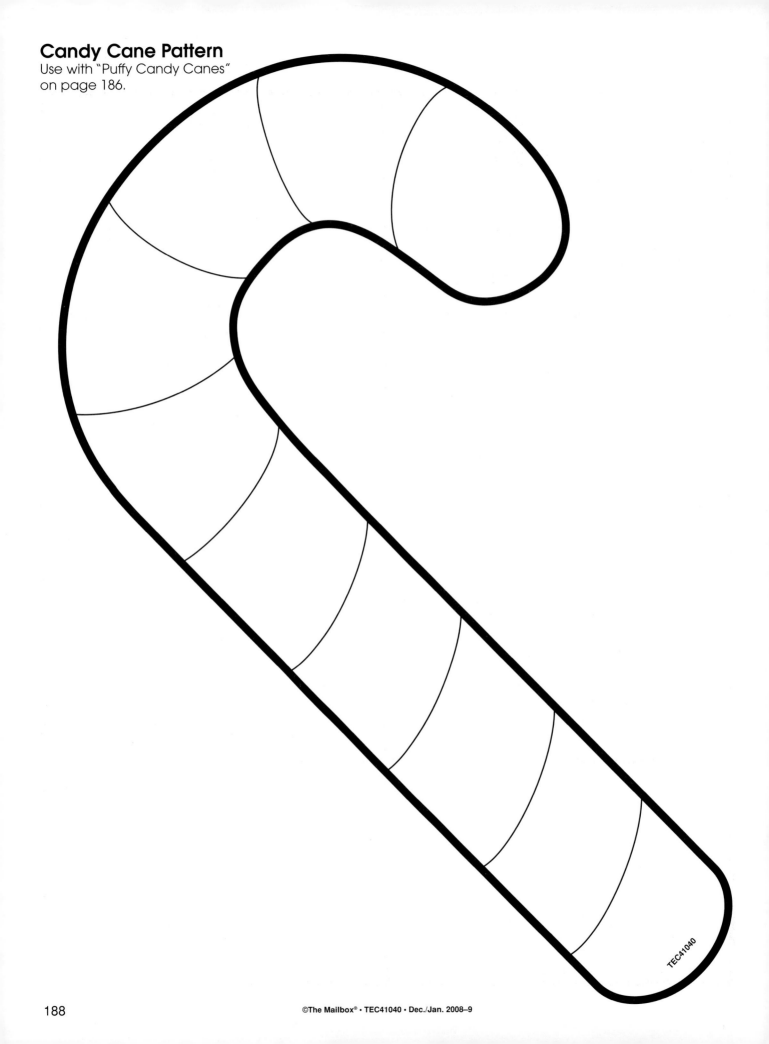

Candy Cane Pattern

Use with "Puffy Candy Canes" on page 186.

TEC41040

TEC41040

TEC41040

TEC41040

TEC41040

TEC41040

TEC41040

TEC41040

TEC41040

Nursery Rhyme Centers

Spotlight classic nursery rhymes
with this fun collection of centers!

*ideas contributed by Ada Goren
Winston-Salem, NC*

Baa, Baa, Black Sheep

Math Center

For this partner game, cut apart a copy of
the bag cards from page 193. Make an adjustable sheep headband with a Velcro fastener.
One child wears the headband and pretends
to be a sheep. His partner asks, "Baa, baa,
black sheep; have you any wool?" The sheep
rolls the die, counts the dots on top and replies,
"Yes, sir; yes, sir; [five] bags full." Then his
partner counts aloud a corresponding number
of bag cards. The partners switch roles, and
play continues. For an added challenge, use
two dice and two sets of bag cards.

Hickory, Dickory, Dock

Block Center

Youngsters dramatize this rhyme using simple props!
Place in your block center a toy mouse, a percussion
triangle, and a clock-face cutout. A child builds a tower to
represent a grandfather clock; then she tapes the clock
face to the structure. She moves the mouse up one side
of the clock as she recites the first two lines of the rhyme;
then she rests the mouse on the top. After she says, "The
clock struck one," she strikes the triangle once. She moves
the mouse down the opposite side of the clock as she
recites the remainder of the verse.

Hot Cross Buns
Dramatic Play

Little ones pretend to make hot cross buns in this mock bakery! Gather items such as those listed below. A youngster molds brown play dough into bun shapes. She uses white play dough to decorate each bun. Then she puts the buns on a tray and pretends to bake them in an oven. Finally, she removes the buns from the oven and pretends to sell them to her patrons.

Suggested materials: light brown and white play dough, aprons, oven mitts, baking trays and utensils, pastry boxes, small brown bags, play money, cash register, receipts, paper, crayons

Hey, Diddle, Diddle
Literacy Center

Youngsters practice sequencing skills with this nursery rhyme favorite. Prepare a copy of the picture cards on page 193 for flannelboard use. Place the cards at a center along with a flannelboard. As a child recites "Hey, Diddle, Diddle," she places the pictures in sequential order on the flannelboard to illustrate the rhyme.

Old Mother Hubbard
Writing Center

Old Mother Hubbard went to her cupboard—and it was bare! Invite your little ones to write a happier ending to this rhyme. For each child, make a brown construction paper copy of the cupboard pattern on page 194. Help her cut the paper along the dotted lines and then glue the page to a sheet of white construction paper, leaving the doors unglued. Help her fold open the doors. Finally, have her write or dictate words to make a new ending to the rhyme. Encourage her to draw the food in the space provided.

Old Mother Hubbard

Went to the cupboard

To fetch her poor dog a bone;

But when she came there...

She found macaroni and cheese!

Mary, Mary, Quite Contrary

Art Center

Mary's garden won't grow without water from her watering can! Make a simple watering can cutout for each child. Help each student decorate his watering can using a marble-painting technique. Then have him tape blue curling ribbon to the spout. These projects look lovely when displayed on a bulletin board with the nursery rhyme text and a row of flower cutouts.

Kara Steinhebel, West Utica Elementary, Utica, MI

Jack, Be Nimble

Gross-Motor Area

With this activity, little ones jump like Jack and more! Color and cut out a construction paper copy of the spinner on page 195, and use a brad to attach a jumbo paper clip to the center. Attach tissue paper to a block so it resembles a flame on a candle. Then place the items at a center. A youngster spins the spinner and then performs the action indicated.

jump

crawl

march

tiptoe

Little Bo Peep

Games Center

Youngsters find Bo Peep's sheep with this simple game! Place index cards in a pocket chart. Then randomly hide sheep cards (see page 195) behind a few of the index cards. A student chooses an index card and removes it from the pocket chart. If a sheep is revealed, he takes another turn. If not, another child takes a turn. Play continues in the same manner until all the sheep are found.

TEC41041

TEC41041

TEC41041

TEC41041

TEC41041

TEC41041

Picture Cards
Use with "Hey, Diddle, Diddle" on page 191.

TEC41041

TEC41041

TEC41041

TEC41041

Cupboard Pattern
Use with "Old Mother Hubbard" on page 191.

Old Mother Hubbard

Went to the cupboard

To fetch her poor dog a bone;

But when she came there...

TEC41041

jump

crawl

march

tiptoe

TEC41041

Sheep Cards
Use with "Little Bo Peep" on page 192.

TEC41041

TEC41041

TEC41041

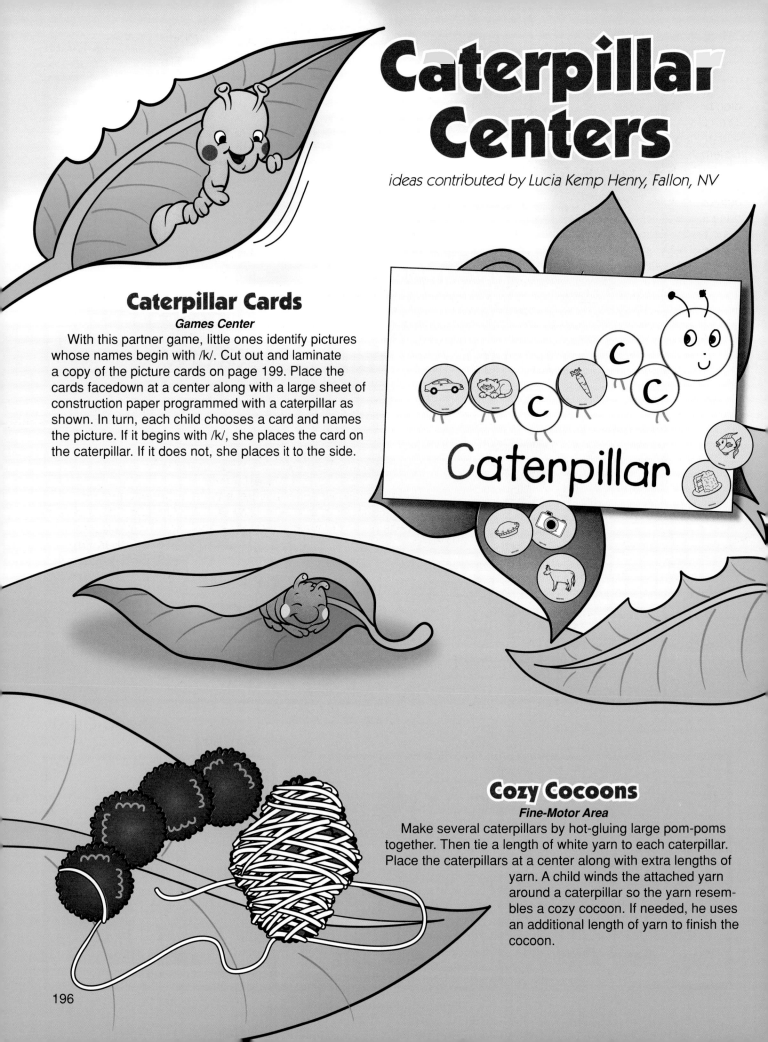

Caterpillar Centers

ideas contributed by Lucia Kemp Henry, Fallon, NV

Caterpillar Cards

Games Center

With this partner game, little ones identify pictures whose names begin with /k/. Cut out and laminate a copy of the picture cards on page 199. Place the cards facedown at a center along with a large sheet of construction paper programmed with a caterpillar as shown. In turn, each child chooses a card and names the picture. If it begins with /k/, she places the card on the caterpillar. If it does not, she places it to the side.

Caterpillar

Cozy Cocoons

Fine-Motor Area

Make several caterpillars by hot-gluing large pom-poms together. Then tie a length of white yarn to each caterpillar. Place the caterpillars at a center along with extra lengths of yarn. A child winds the attached yarn around a caterpillar so the yarn resembles a cozy cocoon. If needed, he uses an additional length of yarn to finish the cocoon.

Munchin' Lunch
Writing Center

In advance, make a class supply of simple accordion booklets. Label the cover of each booklet as shown. Then place the booklets at a center along with scissors and grocery store circulars. Read aloud *The Very Hungry Caterpillar* by Eric Carle. Then invite youngsters to visit the center. A student draws a caterpillar at the top of the first page. Then he cuts out pictures of food and attaches one picture to each page. He dictates the names of the food items for an adult helper to write in his booklet. That's one hungry caterpillar!

What did the caterpillar eat?
By Jacob

bread   cake   chicken   carrots

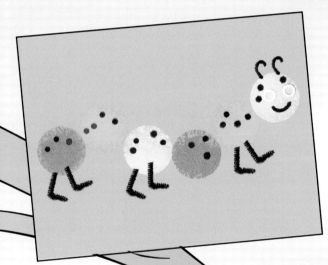

Colorful Caterpillar
Art Center

Place shallow pans of paint at a table along with a round sponge and cotton swab for each pan. A youngster makes several sponge prints on a sheet of paper so they resemble a caterpillar. She uses a cotton swab to make spots on her caterpillar. When the paint is dry, she draws a mouth on her project and attaches hole reinforcer eyes and pipe cleaner antennae and feet.

Scrumptious Leaves
Science Center

This cute idea reinforces that caterpillars eat leaves. Place at a table construction paper leaf cutouts, a supply of paper programmed as shown, three-inch pieces of flexible drinking straws (include the flexible portion), a hole puncher, and glue. A visiting child tears small pieces of paper from the edges of a leaf so it looks as if it's been nibbled on; then she punches several holes in the leaf. Next, she glues the leaf to a sheet of paper. Then she shapes the straw so it resembles a caterpillar and glues it to the leaf.

Caterpillars eat leaves.

Stacie

Caterpillar Names

Literacy Center

For each child, write each letter of her name on a separate circle cutout. Put the circles plus a circle decorated with a caterpillar face in a personalized envelope. Place the envelopes at a center. A visiting youngster locates her envelope and removes the circles. She places the caterpillar head on a flat surface. Then she arranges the circles next to the head to spell her name, using her envelope as a guide. If desired, she repeats the process with her classmates' names.

Andrea Singleton, Waynesville Elementary
Waynesville, OH

Lots of Caterpillars!

Math Center

Youngsters practice identifying numbers and making sets with this idea. Place a supersize leaf cutout at a center along with bingo daubers. Attach a number card to the leaf. A little one identifies the number and then uses the bingo daubers to make caterpillars with the corresponding number of body segments on the leaf. For an added challenge, change the leaf and number card each day.

Very Hungry Caterpillars

Play Dough Center

To prepare for this center, make a supersize caterpillar cutout. Place the caterpillar at the center along with play dough and rolling pins. A visiting child uses the items to make food for the caterpillar; then she pretends to feed it. What a delicious looking caterpillar feast!

TEC41042

TEC41042

TEC41042

TEC41042

TEC41042

TEC41042

TEC41042

TEC41042

Beach Centers

ideas contributed by Ada Goren
Winston-Salem, NC

Beachcombing
Math Center

Your little beachcombers are sure to enjoy this sandy sorting center! To prepare, fill your sensory table with sand. Hide an assortment of beach items, such as seashells and rocks, in the sand. Then provide several hair combs and two plastic pails labeled as shown. A youngster combs through the sand to search for hidden objects and sorts the items into the pails.

Janet Boyce, Cokato, MN

Sunscreen protects skin from the sun.

Ready for Sun
Health and Safety Center

After this nifty center activity, discuss with youngsters the importance of protection from the sun! In advance, copy a class supply of page 202. Place the pages at a center along with crayons, paintbrushes, and pink-tinted water. A youngster takes a page and colors the clothing and scene details. Next, he uses a white crayon (sunscreen) to color the exposed parts of the body and head. Finally, he brushes pink water over the body and head and then blots the page with a tissue. He checks the face, arms, and legs of his drawing. If any parts of the body are pink, he knows he should have added more sunscreen!

Carol Hargett, Kinderhaus III, Fairborn, OH

Lovely Seashells
Fine-Motor Area

Little fingers get a workout with these supersize lacing shells! Cut out and laminate several tagboard shells (pattern on page 203). Punch holes where indicated; then attach a length of yarn to each shell. Place the shells at a center. A student visits the center and chooses a shell. Then she laces the shell using the lines as a guide.

Starfish Toss
Gross-Motor Area

Youngsters work their arm muscles with this fun idea! Place an oversize starfish cutout on the floor. Then place a tape line on the floor several feet away along with a plastic pail containing five beanbags. A child stands behind the line. He tosses the beanbags toward the starfish, attempting to get one beanbag on each arm.

S Is for Sand
Literacy Center

Write the letter S on a class supply of construction paper and place it at a center along with white glue, a paintbrush, seashells, and shallow pans of paint. A youngster runs his fingers over the letter and says its name. Then he brushes glue over the letter and sprinkles sand over the glue. After shaking the excess sand into a trash can, he makes seashell prints around the letter. S is for sand and seashells!

Sunscreen protects skin from the sun.

Note to the teacher: Use with "Ready for Sun" on page 200.

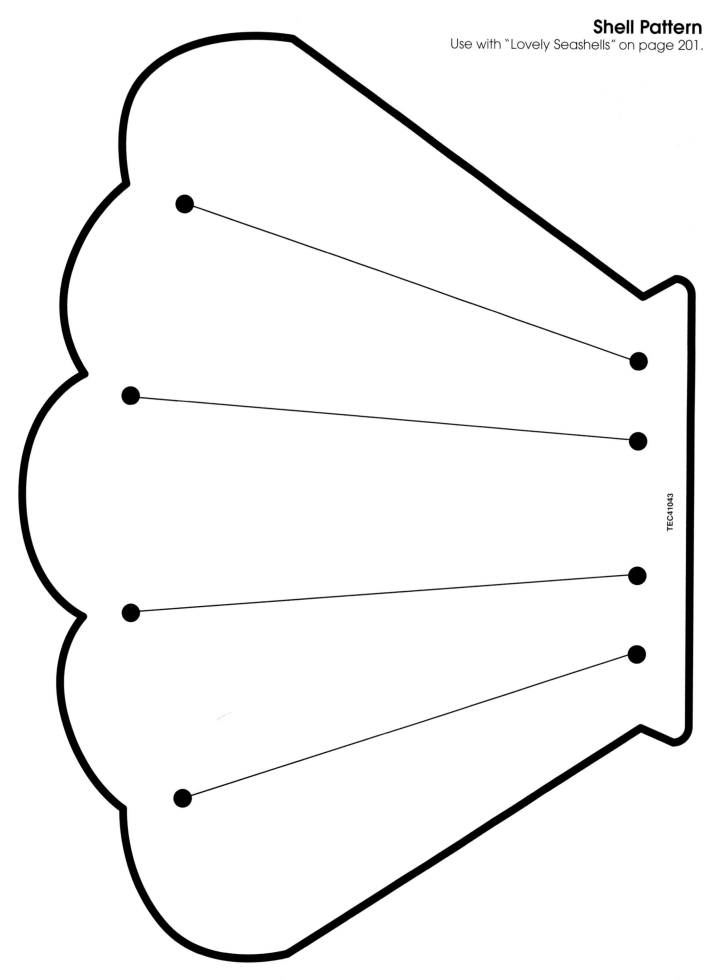

TEC41043

Grocery Store Centers

Little ones will be eager to help with the grocery shopping after engaging in this fun collection of center ideas!

ideas by Elizabeth Cook, St. Louis, MO

Let's Go Shopping!
Dramatic-Play Area

Youngsters engage in authentic learning with this mock grocery store! Stock your dramatic-play area with items from the list below. A youngster looks through a store circular and writes her shopping list. Then she engages in pretend shopping. When she is finished, she pays for her groceries at the checkout counter.

Prop options: toy cash register, play money, pretend credit cards, plastic food, empty food boxes, scale, store circulars, coupons, old receipts, shopping list, notepads and pencils, paper bags or grocery store tote bags

Scan and Bag It!
Gross-Motor Center

Little ones work their arm muscles with this fun partner activity! Attach a black square (grocery scanner) to one end of a long table. Place near the scanner a variety of pretend food items. At the opposite end of the table, place several grocery bags. A student cashier slides an item across the scanner while saying, "Beep," and the bagger picks up the item and places it in a grocery bag. Play continues in the same way until all the groceries have been scanned and bagged.

Checking Receipts
Math Center
In advance, collect a supply of grocery store receipts. Place the receipts at a table along with several highlighters and number cards from 1 to 5. A youngster chooses a receipt and a card. Each time he finds the chosen number on his receipt, he marks it with a highlighter.

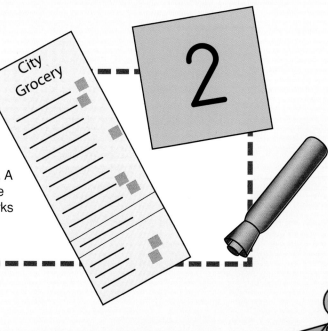

Bakery Delight
Art Center
Cut out a class supply of white construction paper cakes from the pattern on page 207. Place the cutouts at your art center along with markers, bingo daubers, sequins, and glue, as well as a variety of collage materials. Invite a child to decorate a cake with the provided materials. Mount the finished cakes in your grocery store dramatic-play area so it resembles a bakery department!

Double Coupons
Game Center
To prepare for this center, mount pairs of store coupons on separate tagboard cards to make them sturdy. Place the coupons facedown. A youngster turns two coupons faceup. If the coupons match, she places them to the side. If they do not match, she returns them to their facedown position. Play continues until all the coupons have been matched.

What to Buy?
Writing Center

With this activity, youngsters make shopping lists for their delicious recipe ideas! Have a child name foods he would need to purchase to make a particular recipe. Write the recipe name and food items on a copy of page 208. Then encourage him to draw a picture of the finished meal below the list. If desired, bind the completed pages together between two covers and title it "Our Class Book of Recipes."

Shopping List
To make cheeseburgers I will need
hamburgers
cheese
buns
ketchup
tomato
pickles

Letter Match
Literacy Center

Remove the front panels from several cereal boxes and laminate them for durability. Place the panels at the center along with letter cards that match the cereal names. A youngster chooses a panel and finds the matching letter cards. Then he arranges the cards on the table to re-create the cereal name.

Buy It in Bulk!
Discovery Center

Obtain two different bulk food items, such as pasta and rice, and then place them in separate tubs. Label the one-pound mark on a kitchen scale with a sticker. Place the tubs at a center along with a small flat-bottomed container and a scoop. A youngster scoops a food item into the container and places it on the scale. He then adds or takes away some of the food, attempting to get the arrow to point to one pound. He repeats the process with the remaining food item.

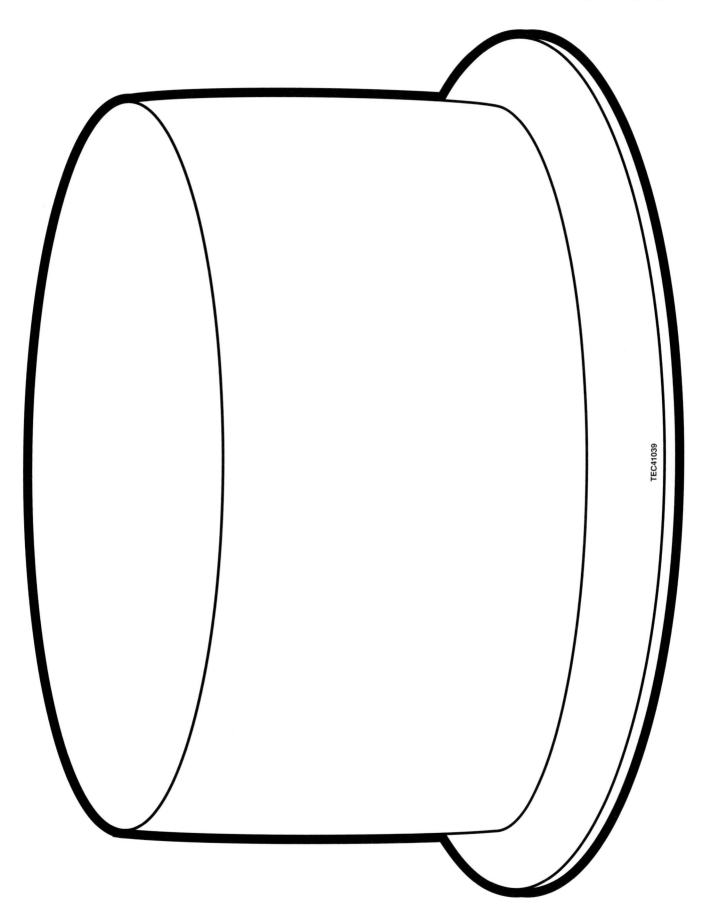

TEC41039

Shopping List

To make _____, I will need

_____

_____

_____

_____

_____

©The Mailbox® TEC41039 • Oct./Nov. 2008

Note to the teacher: Use with "What to Buy?" on page 206.

LITERACY UNITS

Time's I-1y Na .!

What better way to begin the school year than with engaging activities that help little ones learn about their written names!

Living Letters

Youngsters are sure to remember this unique activity throughout their school years. Fill a resealable plastic bag with potting soil and then moisten the soil to make mud. After writing the first letter of each child's name on a separate sheet of cardboard, have him trace his letter with his finger. Then snip a corner from the bag and have the child pipe the mud onto the letter. Encourage him to sprinkle grass seed over the mud. Then place the project near a sunny window. If the mud gets dry, lightly mist the letters. Within a few days, youngsters will see living letters!

Bobbi Chapman
Fiddlesticks Co-op Preschool
Centralia, WA

Make a Match

Use a permanent marker to write each child's name on a separate piece of craft foam. Also write each letter and punctuation mark of each child's name on an individual clothespin. Then store each name with its corresponding clothespins in a separate resealable plastic bag and place the bags at a center. A child finds her name and attaches each clothespin to the corresponding letter. After youngsters have plenty of practice with their own names, encourage them to match clothespins to classmates' names as well.

Patti Ferrick
Child Advocates of Blair County Head Start
Altoona, PA

Seasonal Names

Give each youngster a sheet of construction paper programmed with her name. Then give her two or three markers in colors that correspond to the season. For example, in September you might use fall-related colors and in February you might give her pink and red. Then have her trace over her name several times with each color. If desired, have students attach seasonal stickers around their names. Encourage students to complete a seasonal tracing each month!

Suzanne Maxymuk
Evergreen School
Woodbury, NJ

Letter Hunt

Write the first letter of each child's name on a separate card and place the cards in your pocket chart. Gather student name cards. Hold up a name card and sing the song below, substituting the letter in the song with the first letter in the name. Repeat the song, encouraging youngsters to sing it with you. Then help the youngster whose name you used find her letter card in the pocket chart. Continue in the same way with other name cards.

(sung to the tune of "The Muffin Man")

Have you seen the letter [*G*]?
The letter [*G*], the letter [*G*].
Have you seen the letter [*G*]?
[Grace] needs it for [her] name.

LeeAnn Collins
Sunshine House Preschool
Lansing, MI

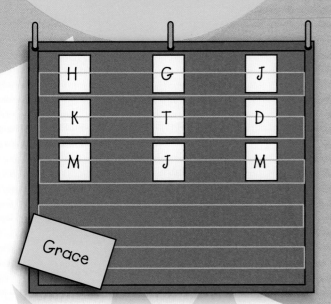

Fairy Dust Names

Dip a paintbrush in white glue and give the paintbrush to a child. Wrap your hand around hers and help her use the paintbrush to write her name on a sheet of paper. Have the youngster sprinkle glitter (fairy dust) over the glue. Then help her shake off the excess dust to reveal her name.

Audra Meyerhofer
Long Beach, CA

Preschool Celebrities

This is a fun way to help youngsters practice writing their names while dismissing them for center time! Explain the practice of people asking celebrities for their autographs. Then say, "May I have your autograph, [Lucas]?" and give the youngster a sheet of paper attached to a clipboard. Have the child use a crayon to autograph the paper. Then have the youngster move on to a center.

Carole Watkins
Holy Family Child Care Center
Crown Point, IN

Beginning Sounds

With this simple chant, youngsters hear that their names share beginning sounds with other words. Hold up a student name card and say the youngster's name. Recite a chant, similar to the one shown, two times, substituting the child's name, the name's beginning sound, and a word that shares the beginning sound. As you recite the chant, encourage youngsters to join in and clap along to the beat.

/t/, /t/, /t/,
Tina, Tina, Tina,
/t/, /t/, /t/,
Top, top, top!

Building Names

Use Con-Tact clear covering to attach the letters of each child's name to individual blocks. Place in your block center a book that shows each youngster's photograph and her name. Then encourage each youngster to visit the block center and build her name and her classmates' names.

Kelly Ash
Waukesha County Head Start
Waukesha, WI

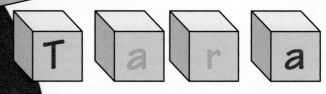

My name is

©The Mailbox® • TEC41038 • Aug./Sept. 2008

Note to the teacher: Periodically throughout the school year, have each child write his name on a copy of this paper. Date the paper and place it in the child's portfolio.

Literacy With Little Miss Muffet

ideas contributed by Lucia Kemp Henry
Fallon, NV

Eeeeeeeeeeeeeeeeeeeeeeeeeeek!!

Act It Out!
Dramatizing a nursery rhyme

Invite youngsters to pantomime this nursery rhyme with a few simple props! To begin, make the simple headband shown, using pieces of Velcro fastener to make the headband adjustable to any head size. Post the nursery rhyme in your large-group area. After youngsters become familiar with the rhyme, encourage a volunteer to don the headband. Have a second volunteer sit on a footstool (tuffet) with a bowl and spoon. Then, as the remaining youngsters recite the rhyme, prompt the volunteers to act out the words.

Laura Sabin, Educational Child Care
Center, Lansing, MI

M Is for Miss Muffet!
Familiarizing youngsters with letters and sounds

Place several letter *M* cutouts in your sensory table along with a supply of white packing peanuts (curds and whey). Color and cut out a copy of the Miss Muffet pattern on page 216 and place the cutout nearby. Provide several plastic bowls and spoons. A child serves up the curds and whey, removing the *M*s. As he places each *M* on Miss Muffet, he says "/m/."

The Spider Beside Her
Listening

Have each child color and cut out a copy of the spider pattern on page 216. Then have each youngster sit on the floor with her spider in her hand. Help students recite the rhyme "Little Miss Muffet," prompting each child to place her spider beside her when indicated. Repeat the rhyme, substituting different positional words, such as *behind, in front of,* and *on,* encouraging youngsters to position their spiders accordingly.

Haha
HeeHee
HeeHee
Haha

Little Miss Who?
Developing phonological awareness

You're sure to hear lots of giggles when youngsters manipulate phonemes with this activity! Help students name a nonsense word that rhymes with *Muffet,* such as *Duffet, Wuffet,* or *Guffet.* Then lead youngsters in reciting the rhyme, replacing *Muffet* with the new word. Repeat the activity several times with different nonsense words.

Miss Muffet's Meal
Writing

To make a class book cover, color and cut out a copy of the Miss Muffet pattern on page 216. Then attach the cutout to the inside of a paper plate along with the poem shown. Give each child a paper plate and encourage her to draw something Miss Muffet could eat instead of curds and whey. Have her name the food item as you write her words on the plate. Stack the plates under the cover and bind the plates together as desired. Then read the book aloud.

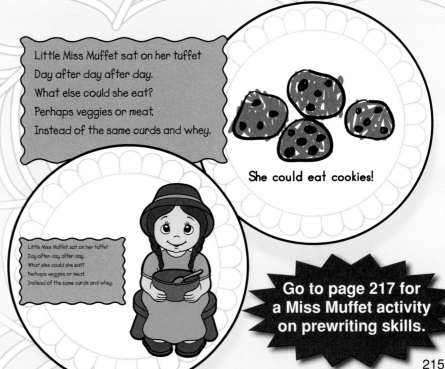

Little Miss Muffet sat on her tuffet
Day after day after day.
What else could she eat?
Perhaps veggies or meat,
Instead of the same curds and whey.

She could eat cookies!

Little Miss Muffet sat on her tuffet
Day after day after day.
What else could she eat?
Perhaps veggies or meat,
Instead of the same curds and whey.

Go to page 217 for a Miss Muffet activity on prewriting skills.

Miss Muffet Pattern

Use with "*M* Is for Miss Muffet!" on page 214 and "Miss Muffet's Meal" on page 215.

Spider Pattern

Use with "The Spider Beside Her" on page 215.

Lots of Spiders!

Note to the teacher: Give a child a copy of this page. Draw a simple spider on a sticky dot and attach it to the top of his index finger. Then have him trace the lines with his finger. If desired, also have him trace the lines with a crayon.

Letters and Sounds

Your little ones are sure to love this selection of soup-themed letter and sound activities. It's just the thing for a cold winter day!

ideas by Ada Goren, Winston-Salem, NC

S Is for Soup
Recognizing the letter s

This alphabet soup only contains one letter—the letter *s!* Place a class supply of page 221 at a table along with a variety of magazines. After familiarizing youngsters with the letter *s* and its sound, have students visit the table and color a copy of the page. Then encourage each child to cut examples of the letter from the magazines and glue them to her soup bowl. That's some splendid, soothing soup!

Ladles of Letters
Matching letters

For this small-group activity, obtain a soup ladle and place magnetic or foam letters in a soup pot, making sure to provide duplicates of many of the letters. Gather a small group of students and ask a youngster to ladle a scoop of letter soup onto the tabletop. Encourage him to find any letter matches in his soup. Have him pretend to eat his soup and then place the letters back in the pot. Encourage each youngster to repeat the process.

Tomato Soup Painting

Forming the letter t

Here's a fun way to form and learn the name of the letter *T*. Place red paint (tomato soup) on a sheet of finger-paint paper. Encourage youngsters to use their fingers to spread the soup. Then prompt them to write capital and lowercase *T*s in the soup. If desired, prompt youngsters to top the wet paint with some soup add-ins, like black confetti (pepper), white confetti (salt), and orange crinkle shreds (shredded cheese). Yum!

No Ps, Please!

Recognizing the letter p

Put a variety of dry pasta in a large soup pot. Then tuck craft foam *P*s in the pasta. Place the pot and a soup bowl at the center along with a pair of tongs. After familiarizing youngsters with the letter *P* and its sound, tell students that you don't want any *P*s in your pasta soup. Then have a student use the tongs to remove the *P*s, saying /p/ as he places each one in the soup bowl.

Soup Ingredient Match

Developing phonological awareness

Make a copy of the soup bowl mat on page 221. Then color and cut apart a copy of the cards on page 222. Place the cards upside down near the mat. Then gather a small group of youngsters. Have a child flip over two cards and say the names of the soup ingredients. If the beginning sounds match, the youngster places the ingredients on the mat. If they don't match, the child flips the cards back over. Play continues until all the cards have been placed on the mat.

What's in My Soup?

Developing letter-sound association

Youngsters make a silly soup recipe with this activity! Provide a soup pot, a mixing spoon, alphabet cards, and a sheet of chart paper labeled with the heading shown. Have a child choose a card and help him identify the letter and its sound. Prompt students to think of a silly ingredient that begins with the letter to add to the soup. When a child names an ingredient, have him drop the letter card in the soup pot and stir the soup. Write the ingredient on the chart paper. After several students have had a turn, review the soup ingredients and then give each child an imaginary bowl of soup!

We're making alphabet soup, and we're putting in

m̲onkeys
b̲asketballs
a̲pples
c̲omputers
t̲ables

Crackers, Please!

Recognizing letters

Attach a supersize soup bowl to your wall. Write several letters on the soup. Then make several square cracker cutouts. Call on a youngster and help him identify a letter. Then have him attach a cracker over the letter. Continue in the same way until all the letters are covered with crackers. If desired, give youngsters a real cracker snack!

Go to page 223 for a soup-themed reproducible writing activity!

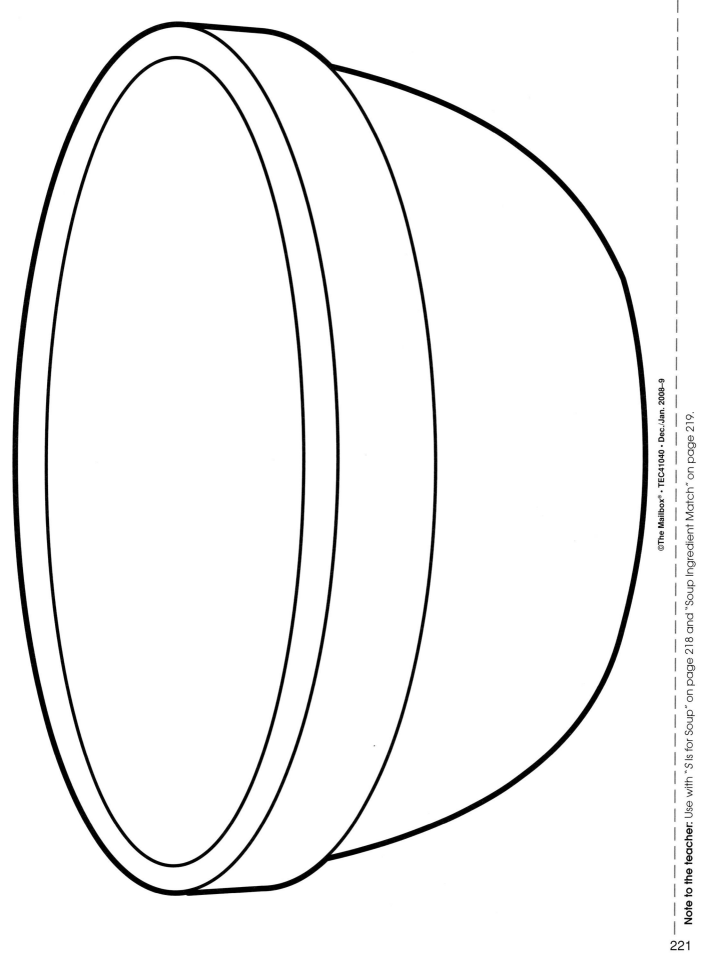

Note to the teacher: Use with "S Is for Soup" on page 218 and "Soup Ingredient Match" on page 219.

Soup Ingredient Cards

Use with "Soup Ingredient Match" on page 219.

TEC41040

TEC41040

TEC41040

TEC41040

TEC41040

TEC41040

TEC41040

TEC41040

Slopping Soup

Lucky Literacy

Your lucky little ones are sure to love this selection of timely St. Patrick's Day literacy activities.

Where's the Gold?

Reciting a poem with rhyming words

Youngsters make a cute little prop to go with this poem. Have each child color and cut out two copies of the leprechaun pattern and one copy of the small pot of gold pattern on page 226. Then help him attach the pot of gold to the end of a jumbo craft stick. Stack the leprechauns, colored-sides out, with the stick between them. Then staple both sides to make a single leprechaun that can be slid along the stick. Lead students in reciting the poem shown, emphasizing the rhyming words. At the end of the poem, have each student hold the leprechaun and slide the stick so the gold pops out of the leprechaun's hat.

adapted from an idea by Brigitte Dade
Helping Hands Preschool, Medina, OH

There was a little leprechaun,
So wise and old.
Now where do you think
He kept his gold?
It wasn't in his house
Or under the mat.
He kept his gold
Up in his hat!

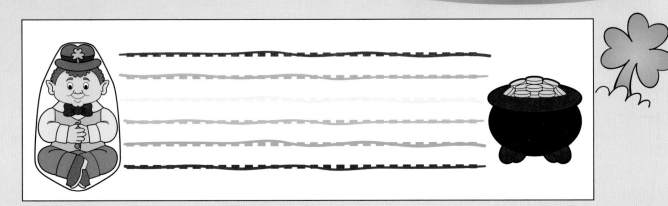

The Rainbow Trail

Tracking from left to right

Color an enlarged copy of the leprechaun and the large pot of gold patterns on page 226. Attach the cutouts to opposite ends of a length of bulletin board paper. Then draw six dashed lines between the patterns. Laminate the paper and place it at a center along with dry-erase markers in rainbow colors. A youngster chooses a marker and practices tracking from left to right by tracing a line from the leprechaun to his gold. She repeats the process for each dashed line.

Tricia Kylene Brown, Bowling Green, KY

224

Searching for L

Recognizing letter L

Scatter letter cards on your floor, including several *L* cards. To begin, lead students in singing the song shown. Then give a child a leprechaun cutout (pattern on page 226). Encourage the child to find a letter *L* card. After you confirm it is indeed an *L*, have him place the cutout over the card. Continue in the same way until all the *L*s are covered.

(sung to the tune of "The Muffin Man")

Can you find the letter *L*,
The letter *L*, the letter *L*?
Can you find the letter *L*
For Lucky Leprechaun?

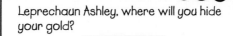

Preschool Leprechauns

Writing

Have each youngster decorate a circle cutout so it resembles her face. Encourage her to glue the circle to a sheet of construction paper programmed with a personalized prompt, similar to the one shown. Then have her glue yarn hair and a hat cutout to the circle. Next, tell the youngster to pretend she is a leprechaun. Then ask her where she might hide her gold. Write her words at the bottom of the paper.

Leprechaun Ashley, where will you hide your gold?

I will hide it in my closet under my toys, and no one will find it.

Leprechaun Pattern
Use with "Where's the Gold?" and "The Rainbow Trail"
on page 224 and "Searching for *L*" on page 225.

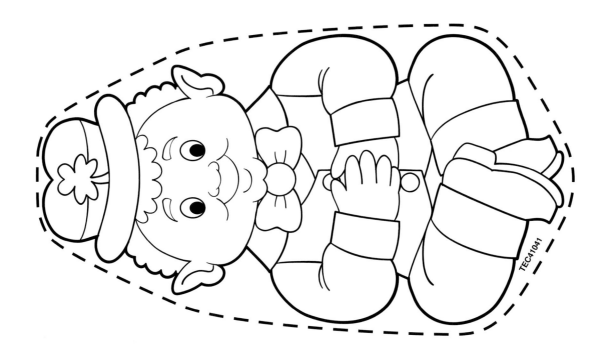

Large Pot of Gold Pattern
Use with "The Rainbow Trail" on page 224.

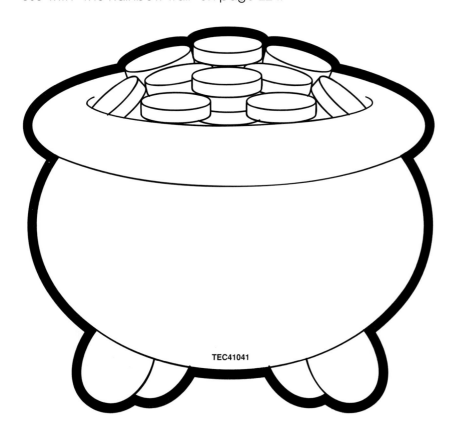

Small Pot of Gold Pattern
Use with "Where's the Gold?" on
page 224.

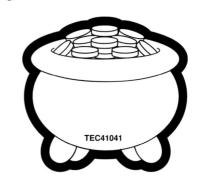

Literacy Is Just Ducky!

Hatching Sounds

Identifying initial sound /d/

Youngsters pretend to be ducks during this adorable phonological awareness activity. In advance, cut out a copy of the picture cards on page 229 and attach each card to a separate egg cutout. Gather a small group of youngsters and have each child sit on an egg. Choose a child and say the rhyme shown. Then have the child hop off her egg and name the picture on it. Help her identify whether the name of the picture begins with the /d/ sound. Then collect her egg. Continue with the remaining youngsters. Then repeat the activity with different eggs.

Hop off your egg with a quack, quack, quack,
And tell us all what picture you see.
Does it begin with /d/, /d/, /d/,
Or something other than letter *D*?

Ada Goren, Winston-Salem, NC

The Ugly Duckling

Writing

Read aloud your favorite version of *The Ugly Duckling*. Then paint each youngster's palm blue, his thumb white, his first three fingers yellow, and his little finger gray. Help him press his hand on a sheet of light blue paper labeled with the story title. When the paint is dry, help him use fine-tip markers to add eyes, beaks, and feet to the fingerprints so they resemble the book characters in a pond. Next, have the student dictate something the ugly duckling might say. Write his words in a speech bubble near the gray fingerprint.

Naoko Aizawa, Cheerful Cherubs Preschool, Greenwood, SC

In the Pond
Forming letter D

For this adorable project, give each child a sheet of paper labeled with a large *D*. Encourage each student to trace the letter with her finger and say the letter's name. Then help her color the space inside the letter so it resembles a pond. Next, have each child press her finger in yellow paint and make a fingerprint on the pond to make a duck's body. Then have her press the tip of her finger next to the body to make the duck's head. Have her repeat the process to make several ducks in the pond. When the paint is dry, help her add details to each duck with a fine-tip marker.

A Ducky Song
Participating in a rhyming song

Lead youngsters in performing this toe-tapping ditty!

(sung to the tune of "I'm a Little Teapot")

I'm a little duck. I say, "Quack! Quack!"   *Point to self; then make quacking motion with hands.*
I have feathers on my back.   *Flap arms as if they were wings.*
Down below I have two big webbed feet.   *Flop feet about.*
They help me swim—aren't I neat?   *Paddle hands like duck feet.*

Ada Goren, Winston-Salem, NC

Webbed Feet
Speaking

In advance, trim orange craft foam into webbed duck feet as shown. To begin, read aloud *I Wish That I Had Duck Feet* by Theo LeSeig. Discuss with students how having animal body parts would change their lives. Then invite a youngster to slip the duck feet over his shoes and explain what he would do if he had duck feet. (If desired, take a photo of the youngster and write down his spoken words to use later for a display.) Continue with the remaining students.

Ada Goren

TEC41042

TEC41042

TEC41042

TEC41042

TEC41042

TEC41042

TEC41042

TEC41042

TEC41042

TEC41042

TEC41042

TEC41042

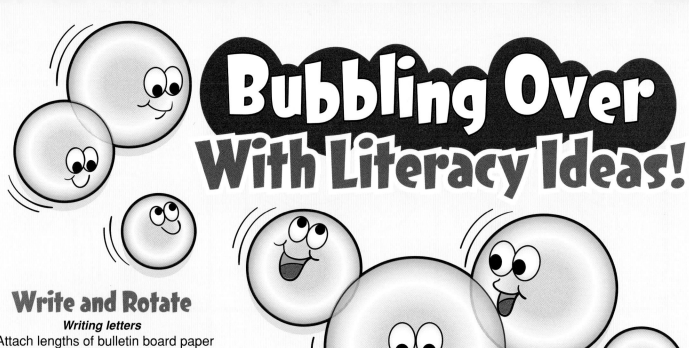

Bubbling Over With Literacy Ideas!

Write and Rotate

Writing letters

Attach lengths of bulletin board paper to four separate tables. Use a marker to write a different letter on each length of paper and then place a variety of different writing utensils at each table. To begin, seat a few students at each table. Have the youngsters at each table identify their letter. Then set a timer and encourage little ones to practice writing the letter on the paper. When the timer rings, remark on all the lovely letters. Then have students stand and move to the next table. Repeat the process until each student has visited all the tables.

Carole Watkins, Crown Point, IN

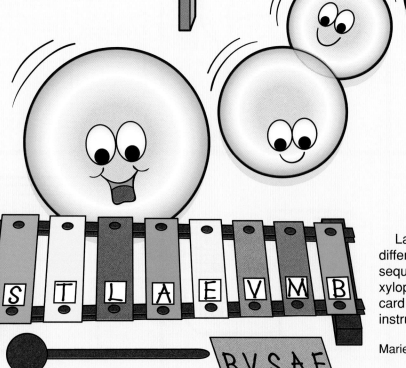

Letter Music

Matching letters

Label the keys of a xylophone with different letters. Then make letter sequence cards using the letters on the xylophone. A youngster takes a sequence card and plays the letters in order on the instrument. What a lovely song!

Marie E. Cecchini, West Dundee, IL

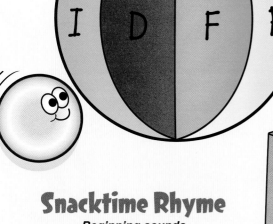

Letter Ball
Identifying letters
Use a permanent marker to write a different letter on each section of a beach ball. Toss the ball to a child and then name a color. The youngster looks for that color on the beach ball and names the corresponding letter. Then he tosses the ball to a classmate. Repeat the process by naming a different color. What fun!

Marie E. Cecchini, West Dundee, IL

Snacktime Rhyme
Beginning sounds
This nonsensical little rhyme can be adapted to work with any letter! While youngsters eat their lunch or snack, chant, "Itsy-bitsy jibbery jee—who has a food that begins with *C?*" Help youngsters identify the sound of the letter *C* and then identify any food they're eating that begins with a *C*. Repeat the process, altering the rhyme as needed. For example, say, "Itsy-bitsy jibbery jess, who has a food that begins with *S?*"

Rhonda Urfey, Allan A. Greenleaf School
Waterdown, Ontario, Canada

Add a Caption!
Writing
Who can add captions to the photos in your class photo album? Your youngsters, of course! Attach your classroom photos to sheets of construction paper. Gather a small group of students and ask each child to describe a photo. Write his words under the photo. Repeat the process until each child has captioned a photo. After laminating the papers, bind them together. Read the book aloud and then place it in your reading area.

Erin McGinness
Great New Beginnings Early Learning Center
Newark, DE

Take a Guess!

Speaking

Write "Take a Guess!" on a box and decorate the box as desired. Then write questions, such as those shown, on separate index cards and place them in the box. When you transition youngsters to a different activity and have a few minutes, instruct a child to choose a card from the box. Read the card aloud and have individual youngsters answer the question. Students are sure to ask for more time with the "Take a Guess!" box.

Sue Reppert, Widening World Preschool
Mentor, OH

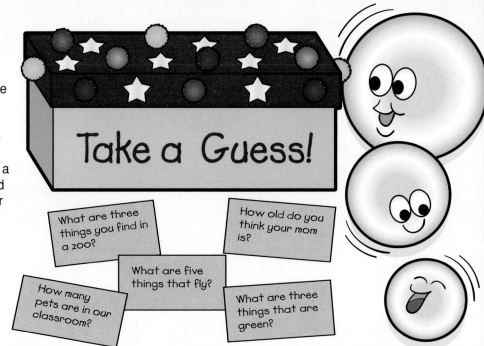

What are three things you find in a zoo?

How old do you think your mom is?

What are five things that fly?

How many pets are in our classroom?

What are three things that are green?

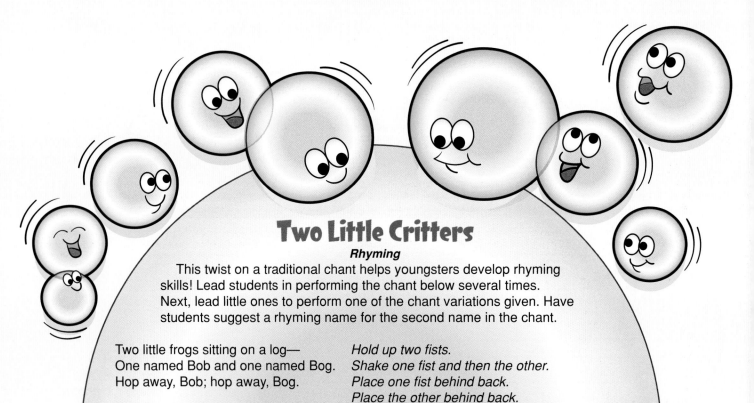

Two Little Critters

Rhyming

This twist on a traditional chant helps youngsters develop rhyming skills! Lead students in performing the chant below several times. Next, lead little ones to perform one of the chant variations given. Have students suggest a rhyming name for the second name in the chant.

Two little frogs sitting on a log—
One named Bob and one named Bog.
Hop away, Bob; hop away, Bog.

Come back, Bob; come back, Bog.

Hold up two fists.
Shake one fist and then the other.
Place one fist behind back.
Place the other behind back.
Bring one fist forward. Bring the other fist forward.

Variations:

bats sitting in a hat—One named Flit and one named [rhyme].
flies sitting on a pie—One named Tim and one named [rhyme].
ducks sitting in a truck—One named Mick and one named [rhyme].
snails sitting in a pail—One named Sip and one named [rhyme].

adapted from an idea by Candy Grzadziel, Elgin, IL

MATH UNITS

Math With Goldilocks and the Three Bears

Three bears, three bowls, three beds, and three chairs—*Goldilocks and the Three Bears* is a tale just meant to encourage math skills!

Are There Three?

Counting

The three bears have three of everything! With this activity, youngsters decide if sets of items belong to the three bears. In advance, gather sets of household items, such as five cups, three toothbrushes, four towels, two shampoo bottles, three pillows, and three combs. Remind youngsters that the three bears had three bowls, three beds, and three chairs. Then present one set of items. Lead youngsters in counting the set. Then ask if the items belong to the three bears, helping students conclude that the items can only belong to the bears if there are three. Continue in the same way with each set of items.

Cindy Barber, Fredonia, WI

So Much Porridge!

Exploring volume

Place uncooked oatmeal (porridge) in your sensory table and provide a cooking pot, measuring cups and spoons, and plastic bowls in three different sizes. Youngsters use the measuring cups and spoons to scoop and pour the porridge into the bowls.

Janet Boyce, Cokato, MN

Small, Medium, Large

Ordering by size

Cut out a copy of the bear patterns on page 236. Also make bowl, chair, and bed cutouts in three different sizes (see pages 237 and 238 for patterns). Attach a piece of felt to the back of each cutout to ready it for flannelboard use. Next, help students arrange the bears, bowls, chairs, and beds on your flannelboard in rows ordered from smallest to largest. Then help students point to the cutouts to retell the story.

Golden Curls

Comparing length

Cut and curl lengths of yellow curling ribbon, making some pieces long and others short. Place the curls in a tub. Then place the tub at a center along with containers labeled as shown. A youngster chooses a curl and decides whether it is long or short. Then she places it in the correct container. If desired, when each youngster has had a chance to visit the center, place the curls back in the tub along with pairs of scissors. Then encourage youngsters to exercise fine-motor skills by snipping Goldilocks's curls.

Janet Boyce, Cokato, MN

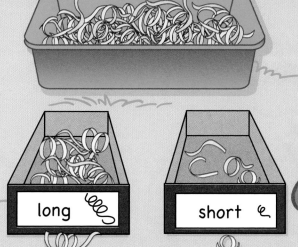

long

short

Tasty or Not?

Organizing data

Place two plastic hoops on the floor and label one hoop with the words "I like it" and the second hoop with the words "I don't like it." To begin, help each youngster pour a packet of instant oatmeal (porridge) into a disposable bowl. Then help him stir warm water into the porridge. After he eats his porridge, have him place a bear counter in the appropriate hoop to show whether he likes or dislikes the porridge. Lead students in counting and comparing the number of bears in the hoops.

Carole Watkins, Holy Family Child Care Center, Crown Point, IN
Linda Tharp, Hickory Child Development Center, Bel Air, MD

TEC41038

TEC41038

TEC41038

TEC41038

TEC41038

Bed Pattern

Use with "Small, Medium, Large" on page 235.

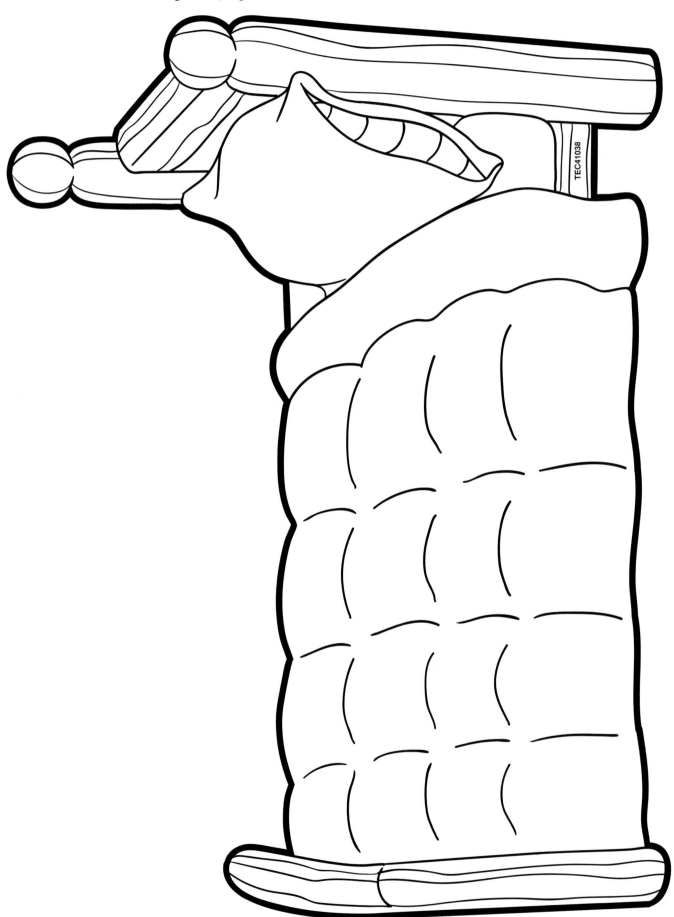

TEC41038

Let's Learn About Shapes!

Shape Cover-Up

This center activity injects creativity into shape identification and formation! Place shape outlines and glue at a center. Also provide different types of pasta, packing peanuts, and pom-poms. A child chooses an outline and names the shape. Then he glues a variety of items around the outline of the shape. How artistic!

Tricia Brown, Bowling Green, KY

Circle or Square?

Little ones are sure to recognize a circle and a square after engaging in this fun activity! Give each child circle and square cutouts. Then lead youngsters in singing the song shown, encouraging each child to hold the appropriate shape in the air when indicated. Repeat the activity several times.

(sung to the tune of "If You're Happy and You Know It")

Hold a circle in the air, in the air!
Hold a circle in the air, in the air!
It is oh so very round.
Hold it high above the ground.
Hold a circle in the air, in the air!

Hold a square in the air, in the air!
Hold a square in the air, in the air!
All its sides, as you can see,
Are the same. Don't you agree?
Hold a square in the air, in the air!

adapted from an idea by Donna Fowler
Forsyth County Public Library, Cumming, GA

Shout It Out!

Store craft foam shapes in a gift bag. (For extra fun, attach eye cutouts to each shape to give it personality). Recite the rhyme shown, looking and reaching into the bag when appropriate. After the final line of the rhyme, pull a shape out of the bag and have youngsters shout its name with great enthusiasm!

I look into my special bag and what do I see?
All kinds of shapes looking back at me!
I reach into my bag and I take one out.
Do you know its name? Then give a big shout!

Gwen Rooney
First United Methodist Preschool
Palm City, FL

In and Out

Cut a large shape in each side of a cardboard box. Then hand a child a small toy and give her directions such as "Put the toy through the circle" and "Take the toy out through the triangle." Repeat the activity until each child has had a turn.

Rebecca Hill
Reeces Creek Elementary
Killeen, TX

Ticket to Ride

Give each of your little train passengers a copy of a train ticket pattern from page 243. To board your passengers, sing several verses of the song shown, each time substituting the name of a shape that corresponds to a ticket. When all the students have lined up behind you, take a short train trip around the room. Toot! Toot!

(sung to the tune of "Down by the Station")

Down by the station early in the morning,
See all the children waiting for the train.
Hear the conductor blow his little whistle.
He shouts, "[Circles] come aboard!"

adapted from an idea by Shelley Hoster
Jack & Jill Early Learning Center, Norcross, GA

Pool Noodle Painting

Cut several pieces from a hollow foam pool noodle. Place the pieces at a table along with construction paper and trays of paint. Have a child make colorful noodle prints on a sheet of paper, helping her notice that the prints consist of an inner circle and an outer circle.

Wanda R. Hostas
God's World Christian Preschool & Child Care
Prescott Valley, AZ

Shapely Trees

Use this activity to reinforce shape recognition and seriation skills! Give each child a set of shapes in graduated sizes. Starting at the top of the paper, have him arrange the shapes from smallest to largest and then glue them in place. Then encourage him to draw a tree trunk below this unique foliage and add any desired decorations.

Marie E. Cecchini, West Dundee, IL

Rebus Song

Program a sheet of chart paper with the rebus song shown. Then lead youngsters in singing the song as you point to the shapes in each line. If desired, invite a student to lead the class in singing the song.

(sung to the tune of "Head and Shoulders")

Circle, square, and triangle, triangle.
Circle, square, and triangle, triangle.
Heart and star and rectangle,
Circle, square, and triangle, triangle.

Shelley Hoster, Jack & Jill Early Learning Center
Norcross, GA

Shape Sculptures

Youngsters create three-dimensional shapes with this idea! Draw shapes on separate pieces of waxed paper. Then have a child dip a length of yarn in tinted glue and place the yarn inside the outline on a piece of waxed paper. Have him repeat the process several times, making sure the pieces of yarn are touching each other. Allow the project to dry for several days; then remove the shape from the waxed paper.

Amy Durrwachter
Kirkwood Early Childhood Center
Kirkwood, MO

On the Move!

Give each child a shape cutout. Then sing the song shown, encouraging youngsters with circles to stand near you and sway back and forth to the song. Repeat the process, substituting a different shape each time.

(sung to the tune of "My Bonnie Lies Over the Ocean")

I'm looking for all the [circles].
I'm looking for all I can see.
I'm looking for all the [circles]
To come make a group with me.
[Circles, circles], come make a group with me, with me.
[Circles, circles], come make a group with me.

Shelley Hoster, Jack & Jill Early Learning Center, Norcross, GA

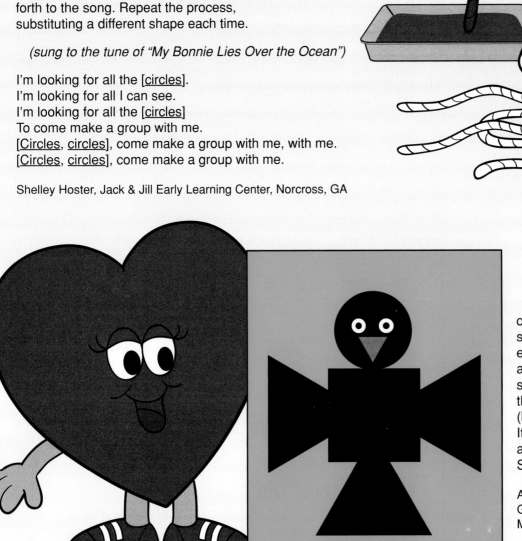

Cute Crows!

For each child, cut from black construction paper a circle, a square, and three triangles. Have each student glue his shapes to a sheet of construction paper as shown. Then have him add to the project a small triangle cutout (beak) and hole reinforcer eyes. If desired, mount the projects on a board with the title "Shapes Are Something to Crow About!"

Angie Kutzer
Garret Elementary
Mebane, NC

TEC41039

TEC41039

TEC41039

TEC41039

Sorting and Patterning With Snowmen!

Sorting Snowman Accessories

Sorting by type

Snowmen certainly need their cold weather accessories! Collect a variety of hats and scarves (or other snowman accessories) and place them in a container. Have youngsters help you sort the accessories into piles by type. Then say, "I want to make snowmen, and I want each one to have a scarf and a hat. I wonder how many I can make." Encourage youngsters to help you rearrange the accessories into piles to find the answer.

It's Melting!

Sorting, patterning

Cut out the snowmen on several copies of pages 246 and 247. Place a snowflake cutout in one plastic hoop and a sun cutout in a second hoop. Then have youngsters sort the snowmen into the corresponding hoops. Next, prompt students to help you attach the snowmen to your board to make an *AB* pattern. As you read the pattern with your little ones, encourage them to stand tall when you say, "Frozen snowman," and to slump to the floor when you say, "Melted snowman."

A Fashionable Snowman
Noticing patterns in real-life objects
Collect some patterned wrapping paper and place it at a table with blue construction paper. Have a youngster visit the table and encourage him to notice the patterns on the wrapping paper. Invite him to draw a snowman on a piece of construction paper. Then have him cut pieces of wrapping paper and glue them to a snowman to make a hat, buttons, mittens, and any other desired accessories.

Elizabeth Cook, St. Louis, MO

Big Nose, Little Nose
Patterning
Obtain a large carrot and a small carrot (snowman noses) and then slice the large end off each nose to make a flat surface. Place the noses at a table along with adding machine tape and a shallow tray of orange paint. A child makes nose prints on a length of tape, as shown, to make a simple pattern.

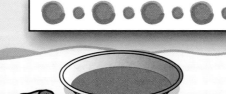

Simple Snowballs
Extending simple patterns
Place a stack of small and large disposable plates (snowballs) near your large-group area. Use some of the plates to create a simple *AB* pattern on your floor. Then ask youngsters what type of snowball would come next in the pattern. Have a student choose the corresponding snowball and add it to the pattern. Continue with several snowballs. Then repeat the process with an *ABB* pattern.

TEC41040

TEC41040

Sweet on Math

Yummy Cherries
Counting

For this small-group activity, provide a die along with a supply of red pom-poms (cherries) on a plate. Have a child roll the die and count the number of dots. Have him remove and pretend to eat the matching number of cherries. Then encourage the remaining students to chant the rhyme below. Play continues until the plate is empty.

> One, two, three, four,
> [Child's name]'s at the cottage door.
> Five, six, seven, eight,
> Eating cherries off a plate.

Denise Crook, Crook Home Preschool, Keller, TX

In the Rhythm
Identifying numbers

Give each youngster a musical instrument. Then hold up a number card. Have students read the number aloud and then play their instruments a corresponding number of times. Continue with the remaining cards.

Karla Broad, Our Savior Preschool, Naples, FL

Take-Home Jar
Counting, sorting

On a large clean plastic jar, attach a label similar to the one shown. Place a note inside the jar asking parents to help their child place a specified number of objects in the jar. Send the jar home with a child, and when he returns it to school, invite the student to share his objects. Then encourage the class to count the objects and determine ways they can be sorted.

Eileen Mattas, Cary Park District Preschool, Cary, IL

Take-Home Jar
Please read the note inside.
Follow the directions.
Return the jar on the next school day.

Brilliant Balloons
Making and comparing sets

Place at a center a class supply of page 251 and several colorful bingo daubers. A student uses a dauber to make a balloon at the top of each string. Then she counts each dog's balloons and circles the dog that is holding more balloons.

Susie Nussbaum, Angie Walter, and Nicole Meyer
Seneca Highlands IU #9
St. Marys, PA

Bunches of Balloons

Phone Number Fun
Recognizing numbers

In advance, write each student's phone number on the front of a seasonal cutout and his name on the back. Distribute the cutouts and have each student place the cutout in front of him so his phone number is visible. Write a numeral on the board and name the numeral. Then instruct any student with that numeral in his phone number to stand. Play several rounds of this activity, choosing a different number each time.

Barbara Carothers Ulmer
Allisonville Christian Church Preschool
Indianapolis, IN

Question of the Day
Organizing data

Use tape to divide your pocket chart from the second row down. Then add the headings shown to each resulting column. Each morning place a sentence strip with a yes-or-no question in the top of the chart. Read the question aloud and invite each child to answer by placing a personalized card in the appropriate side of the chart. After all the students have answered the question, discuss the results.

Kathy McDermott
The Bishop's Academy at Most Holy Rosary
Syracuse, NY

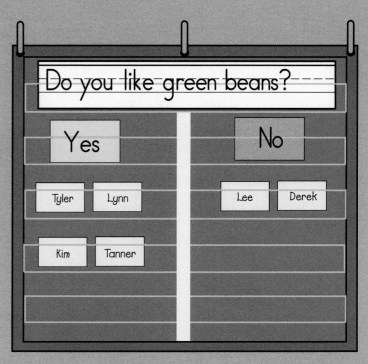

All Kinds of Candy
Measurement
Place at your math center a balance scale along with a variety of wrapped valentine candy. A student chooses two kinds of candy and then predicts which candy is lighter and which is heavier. Then she uses the scale to check her predictions.

Debbie Hoemann, Cleveland Elementary, Norman, OK

Big Bingo
Shape and color recognition
For each student, transform a sheet of poster board into a supersize bingo card similar to the one shown. (Vary the order and color of the shapes on each card.) Gather in a large open area and give each student a card and a supply of beanbags or other large game markers. Have him place his card on the floor and stand in the free space. Name a colored shape. If a student has a matching shape on his board, he places a marker on that square. Play continues until a student has covered all the squares on his board.

Creedence Cathey, Willis, TX

What Can It Be?
Shapes in the environment
Gather a small group of students. Then draw a circle on the board and ask a student to identify it. Draw eyes, a nose, and a mouth on the circle and have another student name what the circle has become. Repeat the activity, changing circles to a wheel, a cherry, and a clock. Then give each student a sheet of paper programmed with a sentence similar to the first one shown and a corresponding shape. Help each child transform her shape into something else. Finally, have her dictate information to complete a sentence about her drawing.

Mary Lou Rodriguez, Santa Cruz, CA

First, it's a rectangle. Now it's a wagon I pull my sister in.

Bunches of Balloons

©The Mailbox® • TEC41041 • Feb./Mar. 2009

Note to the teacher: Use with "Brilliant Balloons" on page 249.

Counting

ideas contributed by Ada Goren, Winston-Salem, NC

Mouse Count
by Ellen Stoll Walsh

A hungry snake counts on eating ten little mice for dinner, but he doesn't count on the mice tricking him and staging a daring escape!

How Many Mice?
Estimating

Get youngsters ready for this read-aloud with a fun visual. Place ten large pom-poms (mice) in a small jar. Explain that you are going to read a story about some mice trapped in a jar. Then have each child hold the jar and guess the number of mice. Write down the students' guesses. Then read the story aloud. After the story, bring out the jar and have students count the mice and evaluate their predictions.

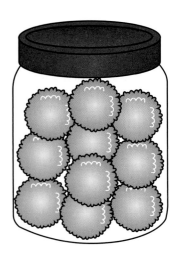

They've Escaped!
Counting

Use the same ten large pom-poms and jar from "How Many Mice?" on this page. Place the jar at a center and hide the mice around the room. Have youngsters visit the center, find the mice, and count them to make sure there are ten. Then have them place the mice back in the jar.

If I were very hungry, I would eat ten pieces of pizza.

Very Hungry!
Making a set of ten

The snake wanted ten mice for dinner! What would your little ones eat for dinner if they were very hungry? Give each youngster a sheet programmed with a large drawing of a jar and the sentence shown. Have her dictate a food item she would like to eat ten of. Then write the name of the item in the blank and have her draw ten of that item in the jar. Yum!

Books

Ten Little Fish

Written by Audrey Wood
Illustrated by Bruce Wood

One by one, each of ten little fish finds other pursuits instead of staying with the school. This simple subtraction rhyme has an ending with an entertaining twist!

Ten and Back Again

Developing interest in the story

To introduce the story, put a fish sticker on each of your fingers. Hold up your fingers one by one as you encourage little ones to count with you from one to ten. Then guide students to count from ten to one as you fold over each finger. Finally, explain that the story you're about to read has ten little fish, like the fish on your fingers!

All in a Line

Participating in an interactive read-aloud

These ten little fish are in a line, just like those in the story! Have each child use a copy of a fish pattern on page 255 to make a stick puppet. Have ten youngsters stand in a line and hold their fish puppets. Encourage the remaining students to count aloud as you point to each fish. Reread the story aloud, encouraging each child to sit down when appropriate. Then repeat the activity with ten different youngsters and their puppets.

Playful Fish

Developing presubtraction skills

Follow up a reading of the story with this fish-related rhyme and activity! Copy the fish patterns on page 255 to make ten fish. Cut out the fish and ready them for flannelboard use. Then attach the fish to your flannelboard. Lead little ones in reciting the rhyme, encouraging a student to remove the number of fish named. Then have youngsters count the fish remaining on the flannelboard. Repeat the process, substituting different numbers.

Ten little fish in the deep, deep sea
Dart and twirl with fishy glee.
[Three] leave the group and swim away.
How many fish are left to play?

Anno's Counting Book

by Mitsumasa Anno

This classic counting book shows the numbers 0 to 12, with a scene to accompany each number. Those skillfully created scenes evolve and include more sets of objects for youngsters to count with each consecutive turn of the page.

Sets of Two
Identifying sets

Before sharing this book with your youngsters, help them identify sets of objects in the classroom, such as four windows, ten manipulative tubs, and one door. Then say, "Now that you have warmed up your counting skills, you're ready for today's story." Read the book aloud, encouraging youngsters to look for and count sets of objects on the pages.

Seek, Circle, Count
Counting

Make this book a part of your math center with the help of a Plexiglas acrylic sheet. Have a piece of a clear Plexiglas sheet cut at a home improvement store. Then open the book on a table and place the acrylic sheet over the book. A youngster uses a dry-erase marker to circle the items in a set. He counts the items to check the number. Then he wipes off the circles and finds a new set of items to count.

A Marvelous Mural
Counting

Youngsters are sure to enjoy making their own counting mural reminiscent of Mitsumasa Anno's art! In advance, make 12 sets of 12 different cutouts. Have youngsters help you glue the cutouts to a length of bulletin board paper, creating their own scene as they go. Display the finished mural so youngsters can enjoy locating and counting the shapes.

Fish Pattern
Use with "All in a Line" and
"Playful Fish" on page 253.

TEC41042

TEC41042

A Great Math Getaway!

Kick back and relax with ideas that require minimal preparation and provide maximum learning fun!

Silent Sets
Making sets

Your little ones are sure to be quiet for this splendid game! Gather magnetic numerals (or numeral cards with magnets attached to the backs) and several decorative magnets. To begin, place a numeral on a magnetic board or cookie sheet. Then tap a child on the head. Have the child silently walk to the board, attach the corresponding number of decorative magnets to the board, and then sit down. Next, lead youngsters in counting the number of decorative magnets on the board. Have them determine whether the number counted matches the numeral. Adjust the magnets as needed and then repeat the game.

Marie E. Cecchini, West Dundee, IL

Mini Ice Cream Cones
Patterning

Label a length of adding machine tape with small ice cream cones. Then attach the tape to a tabletop and provide large pom-poms (scoops) in two different colors. A youngster visits the center and places scoops on the cones to form a pattern. (If desired, provide a sample strip of tape with attached scoops as a reference.) He removes the scoops and repeats the process to form a different pattern.

adapted from an idea by LeeAnn Collins, Sunshine House Preschool, Lansing, MI

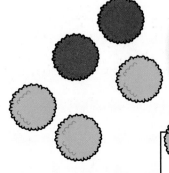

In the Hoop!

Developing preaddition and presubtraction skills

Place a plastic hoop in your circle-time area and gather youngsters in a circle around the hoop. Then give each child five seasonal cutouts. Have each student put one cutout in the hoop as you lead the group in counting aloud. Then have youngsters count aloud again as each child removes his cutout from the hoop. Repeat the process, having each student put in and then remove two cutouts. Keep playing the game until youngsters put in and remove all five cutouts.

Ronda Colbert, The Playplace Preschool, Owensville, IN

Check This Out!

Leslie Timmis of Faith Preschool, Fort Wayne, IN, has a useful tip for helping youngsters distinguish between the numbers six and nine! She simply has them memorize this adorable rhyme: Six has its hand up so it can talk. Nine has its leg down so it can walk.

Splendid Shades

Identifying colors, visual discrimination

Gather a set of four six-ounce soda bottles for each of six basic colors (red, yellow, blue, green, orange, and purple). Fill the bottles with water. Then tint the water in each set of bottles varying shades of the same color. Attach the caps to the bottles and secure them with a little hot glue. Place the bottles at a center. A youngster chooses a set of bottles and identifies the color. Then he arranges the bottles in a row from the lightest shade to the darkest shade. He repeats the process for each set.

Janice Sutherland, Louisiana Schnell Elementary, Placerville, CA

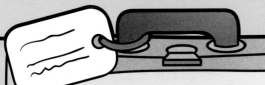

Take It Away!
Developing presubtraction skills
Gather a small group of youngsters and give each child 20 linking cubes. Encourage each child to attach his cubes to build a tower. Then prompt a student to roll a large foam die, count the dots, and remove the corresponding number of cubes from her tower. Have the remaining youngsters repeat the process. Continue until all the youngsters have dismantled their towers.

Karla Broad, Our Savior Preschool, Naples, FL

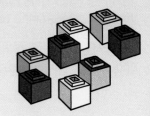

Shape Art
Identifying shapes
Trace a variety of shapes onto construction paper scraps and then place the scraps in a tub along with scissors. Put the tub at a center along with an empty tub. Invite a child to visit the center, choose a paper scrap, and identify the shape drawn on it. Then encourage her to cut out the shape and place it in the empty tub. When the tub is full of shape cutouts, put it in your art center and have students use the shapes for a math-themed collage!

Essra Paddock, Shooting Stars Family Daycare, Warwick, NY

Hungry Shark
Comparing sets
Make a copy of the shark patterns on page 260. Also make several fish cutouts. Attach two sets of fish to your board, making sure one set has more fish. Lead students in counting the sets of fish. Help them determine which set has more. Say, "The shark wants to eat as many fish as he can. Which group of fish would he rather eat?" Then prompt a student to attach the appropriate shark between the sets of fish. Rearrange the fish and play another round of this game!

Karla Broad

Cookie Sheet Sets
Recognizing numbers

Here's a simple center idea! Use masking tape to divide a large cookie sheet into several sections. Then label each section with a different number. Collect a set of objects to match each number and place all the objects in a box. A youngster removes the objects and sorts them. Then he counts a set and places it in the section with the matching number. He continues with each remaining set.

Amanda Russell, Hop-Along Pre-K, La Vernia, TX

How Many Feet?
Nonstandard measurement

This adorable measuring tape is sure to be popular with your little ones! Trim a length of bulletin board paper so it resembles an extra wide measuring tape. Paint the bottom of each youngster's foot and press it onto the paper. When the paint is dry, laminate the resulting measuring tape. Then have youngsters help you use the tape to measure different objects around the classroom.

Missy Goldenberg, Beth Shalom Nursery School
Overland Park, KS

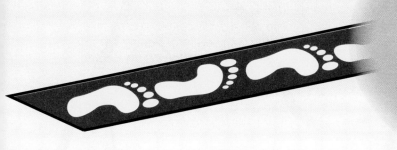

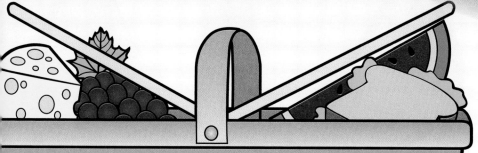

A Number Line
Ordering numbers

Gather a set of number cards from 1 to 20 (or from 1 to 10 for younger preschoolers). Call on a youngster and give him a card. Have him identify his number and then stand in front of the class. Give a second child a number. After she identifies her number, ask her whether the number comes before or after her classmate's number. Then have her stand on the appropriate side of her classmate. Repeat the process for each remaining number card until youngsters have made a complete number line.

Maryann Bennett, North Phoenix Baptist Preschool, Phoenix, AZ

Shark Patterns

Use with "Hungry Shark" on page 258 and "Walk the Plank!" and "A Spiffy Hat" on page 310.

TEC41043

TEC41043

THEMATIC UNITS

WILD About Preschool

Your little ones will give a roar of approval for these wild animal–themed activities and ideas.

Pleasing Animal Prints
Nametags

These nametags are wildly fun and so simple to make! After personalizing a small index card for each child, attach each card to a slightly larger rectangle of animal print scrapbooking paper. Laminate the resulting nametags and punch a hole in each one. Then use a safety pin to attach each nametag to the appropriate youngster's shirt.

Monkeys in the Tree
Getting-acquainted game

Enlarge the monkey pattern on page 65 and make a copy for each child. Then personalize each cutout. Attach a construction paper coconut tree to a wall. To begin, hold up a monkey and help the youngster identify his name. Have the child attach his monkey to the tree. Then lead youngsters in performing the rhyme shown. Continue in the same way until everyone's monkey is attached to the tree.

[Kevin]'s little monkey's in the coconut tree.   *Clap to the rhythm.*
I see it and it sees me!   *Point to self, monkey, and self.*
It says, "Ooh, aah, eeh, eeh, eeh!"   *Scratch underarms.*
[Kevin]'s little monkey's in the coconut tree.   *Clap to the rhythm.*

For a wild welcome-to-school bulletin board featuring fabulous monkeys, go to page 53!

Brilliant Feathers
Craft

This simple craft is perfect for the first week of school. For each child, make a black construction paper parrot cutout and a neon construction paper beak cutout similar to the one shown. Also, cut a supply of neon construction paper strips. A youngster glues a beak to his parrot body and attaches a hole reinforcer eye. Then he glues strips to the parrot so they resemble brightly colored feathers. Display these colorful birds throughout your classroom.

Leslie Watts, New Philadelphia Moravian Preschool
Winston-Salem, NC

See You Later, Alligator!
Attendance display

For each child, laminate an enlarged personalized alligator cutout (see page 65). Then attach the hook side of a Velcro fastener to the back of each alligator. Place the alligators on a tabletop. Then mount a swamp cutout to a wall. Attach the loop sides of the Velcro fasteners to the swamp. When each child arrives, he finds his alligator and attaches it to the swamp. When he leaves for the day, he removes his alligator, places it back on the tabletop, and says, "See you later, alligator!"

Nicole Liversage, San Remo, Italy

Key Countdown
Storytime

In advance, gather six keys and attach them to metal ring. Share the simple picture book *Good Night, Gorilla* by Peggy Rathmann. In this story, a tired zookeeper bids each animal goodnight. But a mischievous gorilla takes the zookeeper's keys and lets each animal out of its cage. Share the story with youngsters again. Each time the gorilla removes a key from its key ring and frees an animal, have a youngster help remove a key from the key ring and set it aside. Count the remaining keys and then continue sharing the story.

"A-peeling" Classroom Jobs
Job display

Write each youngster's name on a separate monkey cutout (see page 65). Also write each desired classroom job title on a separate leaf cutout. Crumple and twist a strip of green bulletin board paper so it resembles a vine. Attach the vine to a wall, as shown, and then mount the leaves above the vine. After adding the title shown, use a clothespin to attach a youngster's monkey below each job.

Monkey See, Monkey Do
Which Preschool Job Do I Have for You?

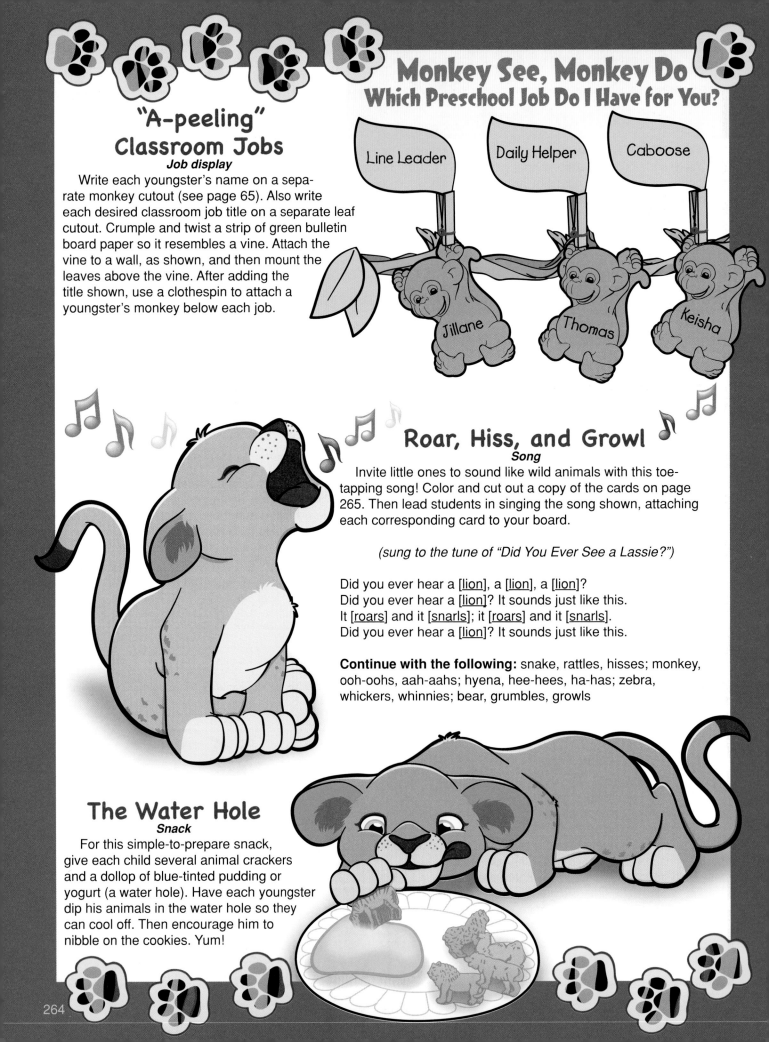

Line Leader

Daily Helper

Caboose

Jillane

Thomas

Keisha

Roar, Hiss, and Growl
Song

Invite little ones to sound like wild animals with this toe-tapping song! Color and cut out a copy of the cards on page 265. Then lead students in singing the song shown, attaching each corresponding card to your board.

(sung to the tune of "Did You Ever See a Lassie?")

Did you ever hear a [lion], a [lion], a [lion]?
Did you ever hear a [lion]? It sounds just like this.
It [roars] and it [snarls]; it [roars] and it [snarls].
Did you ever hear a [lion]? It sounds just like this.

Continue with the following: snake, rattles, hisses; monkey, ooh-oohs, aah-aahs; hyena, hee-hees, ha-has; zebra, whickers, whinnies; bear, grumbles, growls

The Water Hole
Snack

For this simple-to-prepare snack, give each child several animal crackers and a dollop of blue-tinted pudding or yogurt (a water hole). Have each youngster dip his animals in the water hole so they can cool off. Then encourage him to nibble on the cookies. Yum!

TEC41038

TEC41038

TEC41038

TEC41038

TEC41038

TEC41038

Living Things Grow and Change

Here's a lively selection of ideas to help youngsters understand that plants, animals, and people grow and change!

ideas contributed by Elizabeth Cook, St. Louis, MO

Babies Vs. Preschoolers
Making connections between spoken and written words

Help youngsters understand the differences between babies and preschoolers with this cute comparison! Make a two-column chart and label the columns with magazine pictures as shown. Ask youngsters what babies can do and then write their words in the first column. Then ask youngsters what they can do and write their responses in the second column. If desired, extend the activity by adding a third column to the chart with an adult picture and prompting youngsters to share what adults can do.

What can babies do?	What can you do?
They cry.	I can run really fast.
They make diaper messes.	I can slide.
They spit up.	I can make cookies with Mom.
They laugh.	I can jump high.
They grab things.	
They drop rattles.	

From Sapling to Tree
Speaking to recite a rhyme

Introduce youngsters to the term *sapling* with this little action chant about the growth of a tree.

I am a sapling swaying in the breeze.	*Hold up arm and sway it back and forth.*
It's my dream to be a great big tree.	*Continue swaying.*
With a little bit of rain	*Move fingers to imitate raindrops.*
And some sunshine too,	*Put arms over head to imitate sun.*
I'll grow up toward the sky so blue!	*Stand and reach arms upward.*

Baby Animals
Developing vocabulary

Color, cut out, and laminate the cards on a copy of page 269. Attach a piece of felt to the back of each card to ready it for flannelboard use. Then lead students in reciting the rhyme shown as you place each corresponding card on your flannelboard. Finally, have students revisit the name of each baby animal.

We know the names of
baby animals.
Let's name a few!
Pigs are piglets.
Sheep are lambs.
Cats are kittens.
Deer are fawns.
Bears are cubs.
Tigers are cubs.
And lions are cubs too.
Who knew!

I Am
a Living
Thing
by Lia

Living thin

Living things gr

Living things grow stro

Lia
is a living thing.

Who Is a Living Thing?
Developing book awareness

This adorable booklet is sure to be a keepsake for parents. Have each child color a copy of pages 270 and 271 as desired. Then help her follow the steps below to finish each page. When the pages are complete, help her cut them out and stack them behind a construction paper cover labeled as shown. Then bind the pages together as desired.

Page 1: Draw dashes on a construction paper strip so it resembles a measuring tape. Then attach the measuring tape to the page.
Page 2: Place a crumpled piece of yellow tissue paper above each candle to make flames.
Page 3: Trim a piece of a brown paper bag so it resembles a small grocery bag. Then glue it in place.
Page 4: Attach a photograph of your head to the page and write your name in the space provided.

Baby or Big Kid?
Sorting

Gather a variety of items a preschooler might use and a variety of items a baby might use and place them in a basket. Have a student choose an item and help him identify it. Encourage him to determine whether a baby or a big kid would use the item. Then have him place it on the floor. Repeat the process for each remaining item, having youngsters make two piles on the floor: one pile for big kids and one pile for babies.

Let's Move!
Developing gross-motor skills

Youngsters move like babies and like big kids with this simple activity. Obtain an instrument, such as a tambourine. Prompt youngsters to pretend they are babies crawling around on the floor and making baby sounds. Then play the tambourine and encourage youngsters to stand and walk to the beat like big kids. Continue in the same way for several rounds, alternating baby and big kid movements.

Pop-Up Plants
Investigating living things

Have each child draw a sun on a sheet of paper labeled with the words shown. Then encourage her to pull apart a cotton ball (cloud) and glue it to her paper. Next, instruct her to make blue fingerprints under the cloud so they resemble rain. Have her draw a plant on a construction paper strip. Then help her accordion-fold the strip and attach it to her project. As she recites the words on the page, have her pull upward on the plant to watch it grow!

Sun and rain make plants grow!

TEC41038

TEC41038

TEC41038

TEC41038

TEC41038

TEC41038

TEC41038

2

Living things grow older.

1

Living things grow bigger.

4

is a living thing.

3

Living things grow stronger.

Splendid Scarecrows!

Wow your youngsters with these fun scarecrow and corn–themed activities!

Cute Crafts
Identifying shapes

These adorable scarecrows are sure to look fantastic displayed in your classroom! For each youngster, prepare the following cutouts: a square (body), 4 rectangles (arms and legs), a circle (head), a large triangle (hat), and a small triangle (nose). Have each child glue the nose to the head and draw additional features. Then encourage her to glue the cutouts together, as shown, identifying each shape as she works. Next, have her glue to the resulting scarecrow square cutouts (patches) and construction paper strips (straw). Finally, instruct her to add any desired details.

Janis Green, St. Elizabeth School, Cambridge, Ontario, Canada

Fly Away, Crows!
Developing gross-motor skills

Gather youngsters around a parachute (or bedsheet). Have students count ten simple crow cutouts as you place them on the parachute. Encourage each child to grab the edge of the parachute. Then lead students in performing the rhyme below.

Ten black crows flew out one morn.	*Walk clockwise.*
They circled around the fields of corn.	*Continue walking.*
The wind woke the scarecrow; it started to shake	*Stop and shake slightly.*
To show those crows they'd made a mistake.	*Continue shaking.*
It scared them away when the cold wind blew.	*Crouch down.*
It scared them away and off they flew!	*Stand and lift parachute, tossing crows.*

Deborah Davenport-Gibbone, Springfield, PA

Scarecrow Joe
Developing listening skills

No doubt this circle-time activity will be popular with your youngsters! Transform a tagboard copy of the scarecrow on page 276 into a stick puppet. Seat youngsters in a circle and give a child the puppet. Recite the rhyme shown, encouraging youngsters to pass the scarecrow to their right each time they hear the word *pass.* Keep repeating the rhyme until the scarecrow makes it around the circle.

Where did you come from, where did you go?
Where did you come from, Scarecrow Joe?
Pass the scarecrow to a friend.
Pass it round and round again.

Deborah Davenport-Gibbone, Springfield, PA

Cornmeal Play Dough
Developing fine-motor skills

If desired, have little ones help make this no-cook play dough! Place in a mixing bowl 2½ cups of flour, one cup of cornmeal, one tablespoon of oil, one cup of water, and a few drops of yellow food coloring. Stir the mixture until combined and then knead the dough thoroughly, adding oil as needed to reach the desired consistency. Place the dough in a center for youngsters to explore.

Marie E. Cecchini, West Dundee, IL

The Little Old Lady Who Was Not Afraid of Anything

by Linda Williams   illustrated by Megan Lloyd

No Fear Here!
Participating in an interactive read-aloud

Read aloud *The Little Old Lady Who Was Not Afraid of Anything* by Linda Williams. In this story, an old lady walks home one night and is followed by clomping, wiggling, shaking clothing and an enormous jack-o'-lantern. Now she has the makings for a fabulous scarecrow! After the reading, give each child a piece of clothing to match one of the clothing items in the story. Then read the story once again, encouraging students to wiggle and shake their props appropriately. What fun!

Marcia Wuest
Messiah Lutheran Preschool
Port Byron, IL

It's Made From Corn!
Investigating plants
Youngsters are sure to be intrigued by this discovery center! Place at a table ears of feed corn, fresh sweet corn, and Indian corn. Also provide samples of different corn products, such as cornflakes, cornstarch, cornmeal, corn oil, and corn syrup. Place magnifying glasses nearby. Then encourage youngsters to visit the center to explore the items.

Marie E. Cecchini, West Dundee, IL

Who Took the Button?
Identifying one's name
Show youngsters a copy of the scarecrow on page 276 and tell students that its button is missing. Hold up a student name card and have the child identify his name. Then lead him in the chant shown. After each child has an opportunity to participate in the chant, recite the ending below, encouraging youngsters to pantomime the words.

Teacher: Who took the button off the scarecrow's shirt?
[Student name] took the button off the scarecrow's shirt!
Child: Who, me?
Teacher: Yes, you!
Child: Couldn't be!
Teacher: Then who?

Ending chant:
Who took the button off the scarecrow's shirt?
The wind blew—the button flew!
And that's the story—I'm sure it's true.

Marcia Wuest, Messiah Lutheran Preschool, Port Byron, IL

Corn Sensory Bags
Developing the sense of touch
Place kernels of feed corn in a heavy-duty resealable plastic bag along with several squirts of tempera paint. Close the bag and secure the opening with tape. Make several bags in this manner and place them at your sensory center. A youngster visits the center and squishes and squeezes the bags.

Hayley Hanson, Little Acorns Child Care, Long Lake, MN

What Does the Scarecrow See?
Contributing to a class book

Have each youngster color and cut out a copy of the scarecrow pattern on page 276. Also have him cut out a copy of the class book strips on page 277. Then instruct him to attach the scarecrow and strips to a sheet of construction paper as shown. Next, ask him what the scarecrow might see in the fall and write his word(s) in the space provided. Finally, have him draw a picture below his dictation. Bind the pages together with a cover and then read aloud this class-made book.

Danielle Morris, ECSE Preschool at Lodoen, West
   Fargo, ND

Scarecrow, scarecrow, what do you see?

I see a ___pumpkin___,
Fiddle dee dee!

Shoo!
Participating in a song

Have each child place a scoop of popcorn kernels in a plastic container. Secure the lid with tape. Then lead youngsters in singing the song shown, encouraging them to shake their containers each time they say the word *shoo.* After the performance, gather the shakers for safekeeping.

(sung to the tune of "Shoo Fly")

Shoo, crows, don't bother me!
Shoo, crows, don't bother me!
Shoo, crows, don't bother me,
This field of corn is mine, you see.
I am, I am, I am,
I am a big scarecrow.
I am, I am, I am,
I am a big scarecrow.
Shoo, crows, don't bother me!
Shoo, crows, don't bother me!
Shoo, crows, don't bother me,
This field of corn is mine, you see.

Amy Durrwachter, Kirkwood Early Childhood Center, Kirkwood, MO
Shelley Hoster, Jack & Jill Early Learning Center, Norcross, GA

Scarecrow Pattern

Use with "Scarecrow Joe" on page 273, "Who Took the Button?" on page 274, and "What Does the Scarecrow See?" on page 275.

TEC41039

Scarecrow, scarecrow, what do you see?

TEC41039

I see a _____.
Fiddle dee dee dee!

HOLIDAY TRADITIONS

Baking cookies for Santa, lighting the menorah, and placing poinsettias around the home–there are so many different holiday traditions! Help youngsters recognize different traditions with this festive selection of activities!

Holiday Countdown
Counting, identifying numbers

Many people enjoy counting down the days until the holidays arrive! To make this countdown display, decide the number of days you wish your countdown to last; then collect an equal number of old holiday cards. Remove the backs from the cards and then attach the remaining pictures to a wall. Place a number card over each picture to make a countdown. Each day, have a youngster remove one of the number cards, revealing the picture underneath. When a student removes number one, it's time for the holidays!

Randi Austin, Stoutland R-2 Elementary, Stoutland, MO

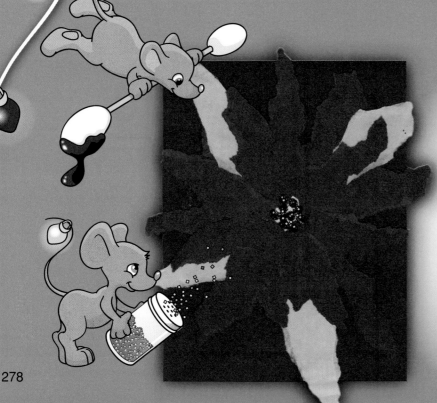

Pleasing Poinsettia
Developing fine-motor skills

Gather a small group of youngsters and explain that some people purchase lovely holiday plants called poinsettias. Show youngsters a photograph of a poinsettia. Then have each child glue a yellow circle cutout to a sheet of construction paper. Encourage her to tear green and red (or pink) paper and then glue the resulting leaves and petals around the circle. Help each child dip a cotton swab into black paint and make several dots on the yellow circle. Then have him sprinkle glitter over the paint.

Holiday Tree Trunks
Investigating living things

For many people, purchasing a live holiday tree is a tradition. Encourage youngsters' families to send in small pieces of the tree trunk that were removed before the tree was placed in a stand. Place the pieces of trunk at a center along with magnifying glasses, tweezers, color paddles, and other tools. Then invite youngsters to the table to investigate the tree trunk pieces.

Marie E. Cecchini
West Dundee, IL

Kwanzaa Fruit
Appreciating similarities and differences among people

Families who celebrate Kwanzaa often display a basket of fruit among other Kwanzaa symbols. Present a basket of fruit. Explain that the fruit reminds people of the importance of hard work. Growing fruit is hard work, but the tasty fruit is a reward at the end. Have students explore and identify the fruit. Then give each youngster a snack of mixed fruit to celebrate hard work!

Deborah Garmon, Groton, CT

Light the Candles
Reciting a rhyme

Many people light fragrant candles during the holidays. Have youngsters celebrate this tradition with an adorable fingerplay!

Let's light the candles,	Hold up fist.
One, two, three.	Hold up three fingers, one at a time.
Place them on the mantel	Wave fingers back and forth.
For all to see.	
When it's time for bed	Rest cheek on hands and close eyes.
And our day is done,	
Blow them out,	Hold up three fingers.
Three, two, one.	Blow on a different finger after each word.

Roxanne LaBell Dearman, Western NC Early Intervention Program for Children Who Are Deaf or Hard of Hearing, Charlotte, NC

Cookies For Santa

Sequencing events

No doubt Santa is happy that this tradition is common in many households! In advance, color and cut out a copy of the cards on page 282 and ready them for flannelboard use. As you lead youngsters in singing each verse of the song below, attach the corresponding card to your flannelboard and prompt youngsters to pantomime the action. After the song, scramble the cards and then have youngsters reorder them.

(sung to the tune of "Peanut Butter and Jelly")

[<u>First, you take the batter and you stir it, you stir it.</u>]
[<u>First, you take the batter and you stir it, you stir it.</u>]
Cookies, Christmas cookies, for Santa!
Cookies, Christmas cookies, for Santa!

Continue with the following:
Then you take the dough and you roll it, you roll it.
Then you take the cutters and you press them, you press them.
Then you take the shapes and you bake them, you bake them.
Then you take some frosting and you spread it, you spread it.
Then you take some sprinkles and you shake them, you shake them.

Roxanne LaBell Dearman, Western NC Early Intervention Program
for Children Who Are Deaf or Hard of Hearing, Charlotte, NC

Acts of Kindness

Listening

Help youngsters recognize that acts of kindness and goodwill are important holiday traditions for many individuals. Have students listen carefully as they help you make a batch of simple cookies or other treats. Encourage youngsters to help you place the cooled cookies in holiday treat bags. Then use curling ribbon to attach the poem shown to each bag. Have students deliver the treats to teachers and staff members at your school.

Lynne Cucco, Little Paws Preschool, Frenchtown, NJ

We're spreading lots of kindness
In all we do and say.
A random act of kindness,
We share with you today.

Tree Trimming
Developing fine-motor skills

People who celebrate Christmas often trim a holiday tree. Place a class supply of green triangle cutouts at your art center along with glue and a variety of paper scraps and craft items. Encourage each child to use the items to decorate a triangle. When the glue is dry, mount the triangles on a wall in the formation shown. (You or your youngsters may need to make extra triangles to fill in any spaces.) Then add a trunk and star cutout to the display.

Beth Marquardt, St. Paul's School of Early Learning, Muskego, WI

Menorah Construction
Developing spatial skills

Youngsters recreate the tradition of lighting the Hanukkah menorah with this block center. Use blocks to construct a simple menorah and candles similar to the one shown. Take a photograph of your menorah. Then enlarge the photo and place it at your block center. A youngster looks at the photo and builds a menorah. Then he "lights" the menorah by placing a small block on each candle.

Janet Boyce, Cokato, MN

Strings of Lights
Sorting

Make a supply of colorful lightbulb cutouts (see page 283). To begin, plug a string of holiday lights into an outlet. Then have students observe the lights while they discuss whether their families use strings of lights to decorate their homes. Next, have each child choose a bulb cutout in his favorite color. Help youngsters sort the cutouts onto different lengths of green yarn so they resemble strings of lights. Finally, have youngsters compare the number of lights on each string.

Christine Vohs
Blue Valley Montessori
Overland Park, KS

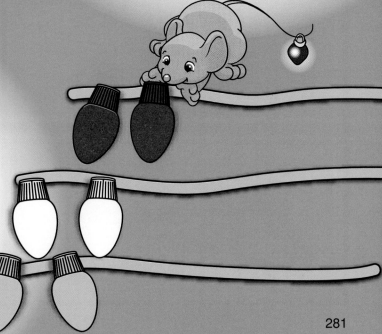

Sequencing Cards

Use with "Cookies for Santa" on page 280.

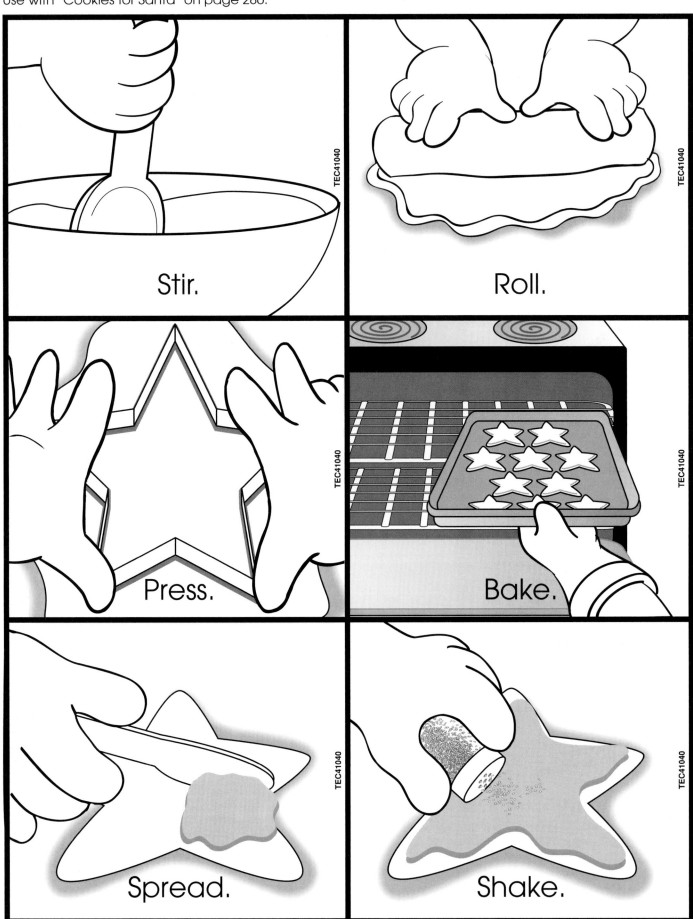

Stir.

Roll.

Press.

Bake.

Spread.

Shake.

TEC41040

Lightbulb Patterns

Use with "Strings of Lights" on page 281 and "Letter and Number Lights" on page 88.

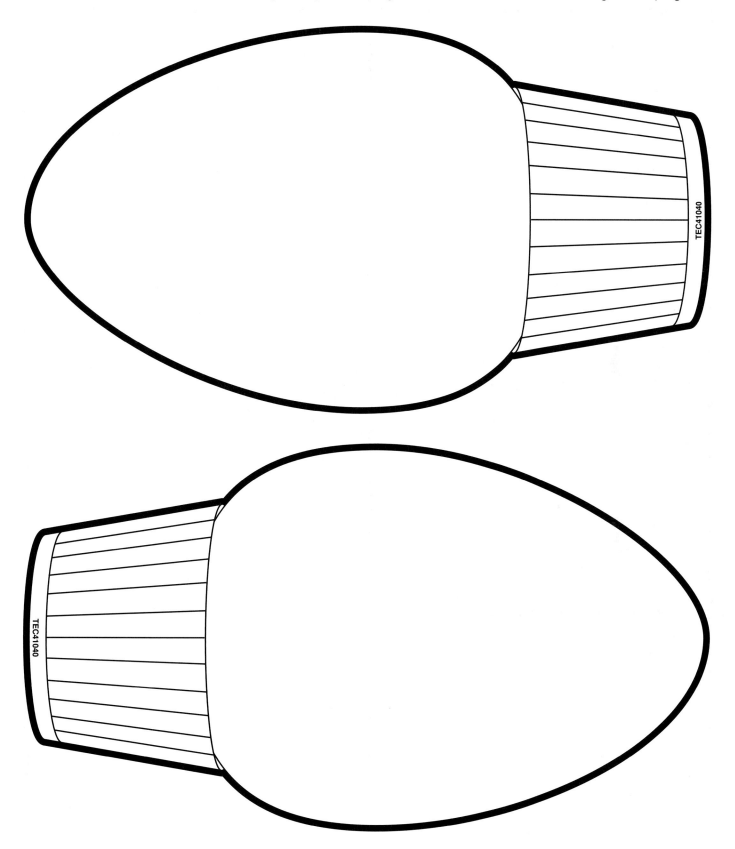

TEC41040

TEC41040

Celebrating Our Differences

Inspire youngsters to celebrate diversity with this selection of fun ideas!

ideas contributed by Lucia Kemp Henry, Fallon, NV

What's Different?

Introduce the concept of differences with this simple game. Invite a volunteer to stand in front of the group. After his classmates have had a moment to study him, remove him from their view and help him change his appearance in a couple of ways, such as by putting on mittens, changing shoes, or putting on sunglasses. Next, emphasize that the child looks different from the way he looked before. Then help students identify the differences. Repeat this game several times with different volunteers.

Tabitha Wiggins
New Adventure Learning Center
Brevard, NC

Delightfully Different!

Here's an adorable song that helps youngsters celebrate differences among people. To begin, lead youngsters to share ways they are both the same and different from their classmates. You might focus on hair color, eye color, skin color, and height. Then lead a discussion about how individual differences make each person unique. Finally, help students celebrate diversity by leading them in singing the song shown.

(sung to the tune of "Have You Ever Seen a Lassie?")

Everyone of us is different.
We're different, we're different.
Let's celebrate the differences
Between you and me.

Our hair and our eyes
And our skin and our size,
Let's celebrate the differences
Between you and me!

I have blue eyes, and Collin has brown eyes.

Fabulous Fingerprints

Students learn that fingerprints are one of a kind with this unique idea! Give each child a die-cut hand programmed with her name. Help her press a fingertip onto an ink pad and then onto the corresponding finger of her die-cut hand. Repeat the process with each remaining finger. Then invite students to use a magnifying glass to observe and compare the fingerprints. Help each child understand that everyone's fingerprints are different.

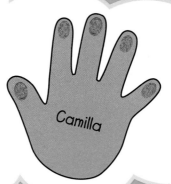

Special Me

Little ones share what makes them unique with this fun idea! Play a recording of lively music and have youngsters pass a handheld mirror around the circle. When you stop the music, the child holding the mirror looks in it and completes the sentence "I am special because…" Encourage students to think of attributes other than appearance, such as being kind to others and being a fast runner! Continue until each child has had the chance to share what makes him special.

Unique Keepsake

Make a construction paper copy of page 286 for each child. (Enlarge the page if necessary). Have her make handprints on each side of the poem. Then encourage her to glue a photograph of her face above the poem. Send these cute keepsakes home to parents or bind them in a class book for your reading center.

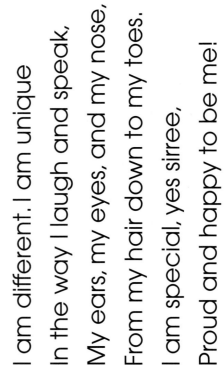

I am different. I am unique
In the way I laugh and speak,
My ears, my eyes, and my nose,
From my hair down to my toes.
I am special, yes sirree,
Proud and happy to be me!

Note to the teacher: Use with "Unique Keepsake" on page 285.

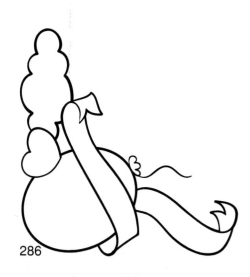

Delightful Dinosaurs

Bones and Claws
Sorting

Use common pasta shapes for this simple sorting center! Place penne pasta (dinosaur bones) and elbow macaroni (dinosaur claws) in your sand table. Label sorting containers as shown and then place them nearby. Provide tools such as tweezers and sieves. A youngster visits the center and uses the tools to find bones and claws, and then he sorts them into the appropriate containers.

Antoinette Cesiro, Hopewell Junction, NY

bones

claws

Little Stegosaurus

Participating in a song

Have each child transform a copy of the dinosaur patterns from page 290 into stick puppets. Lead youngsters in the song shown, prompting them to use their puppets to pantomime the dinosaurs' interactions. Sing the song two more times, reducing the underlined number each time. After the final round of singing, have youngsters pantomime the *Stegosaurus* running far away from the *T. rex*.

(sung to the tune of "Little Bunny Foo Foo")

Little *Stegosaurus* tromping through the forest,
Munching on the green plants from morning until night.

Down came a *T. rex,* and it said,
"Little *Stegosaurus*,
"I don't want to see you
"Munching all the green plants from morning until night.
"I'll give you [three chances],
"And if you don't do as I say,
"I'm going to have you for dinner—yum, yum, yum!"

Lisa Quinones, Family Life Program, Downer Grove, IL

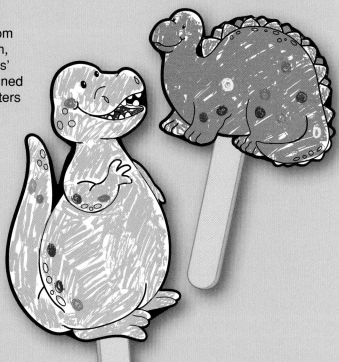

Check This Out!

To create an engaging display for a dinosaur theme, Irene Castell of Bethany Learning Center, Broken Arrow, OK, attaches a path of dinosaur footprint cutouts leading to her classroom door. Then she decorates the door with caution tape purchased at a home improvement store.

"Tricera-toss"
Developing gross-motor skills
This gross-motor game is easy to prepare! Make a simple *Triceratops* head cutout. Place the head on the floor and then place three physical education cones (or weighted two-liter soda bottles) on the head so they resemble horns. Trim the center from several sturdy disposable paper plates to make tossing rings and place them nearby. A youngster stands several feet from the *Triceratops* and attempts to toss the rings around the horns.

Kimberly Curry, Cunningham Creek Elementary, Jacksonville, FL

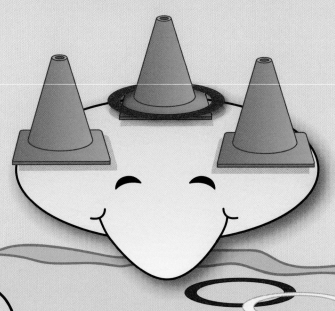

Meat Eater, Plant Eater
Investigating living things from the past
Enlarge the patterns on page 290 and then make a construction paper copy of each one. Attach the dinosaur cutouts to a wall. Explain that the *Stegosaurus* was a plant eater and the *Tyrannosaurus rex* was a meat eater. Then encourage youngsters to cut meat and plant pictures from magazines and grocery store flyers and glue each one to the appropriate dinosaur.

Marie E. Cecchini, West Dundee, IL

Big Feet!
Estimation
Cut from bulletin board paper a circle with a one-yard diameter. Then gather youngsters around the circle. Explain that the cutout is about the size and shape of an *Apatosaurus* footprint. If possible, share a picture of an *Apatosaurus.* Then ask youngsters to guess how many students could sit on the footprint. After students share their guesses, prompt several youngsters to sit on the footprint as the remaining students count aloud. When the print is full, count the total number of students and have youngsters compare the number to their estimates.

Betsianne Bench, Galion, OH

Give a Roar!
Matching letters

Label pairs of dinosaur cutouts (patterns on page 290) with matching letters. Then scatter the dinosaurs on the floor and have students form a circle around the dinosaurs. Next, lead your little ones in singing the song as they stomp around the circle. Prompt them to sit down. Then have one child choose a dinosaur and name the letter. Encourage a second child to find a dinosaur with the matching letter. Then have the remaining youngsters give a roar of approval! Continue for several rounds.

(sung to the tune of "This Old Man")

Dinosaur, give a roar.
Find a letter on the floor.
Pick it up now, please.
Then you can say its name.
Find the one that looks the same.

Karianne Sis, Hearne Elementary, Houston, TX

Little Paleontologists
Developing fine-motor skills

In advance, mix plaster of paris according to package directions. Then pour a layer of the mixture into a plastic tub. As the plaster begins to harden, press plastic dinosaurs into the mixture; then remove the dinosaurs. When the plaster has hardened completely, pour a layer of sand over the plaster. Place the tub at a center along with magnifying glasses, paintbrushes, and dinosaur books. Your little paleontologists visit the center and use the items to reveal and study these homemade fossils.

Irene Castell, Bethany Learning Center, Broken Arrow, OK

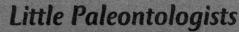

Apatosaurus

Plesiosaurus

For extra dinosaur fun, cut out several copies of the dinosaur cards on page 291 and have youngsters use them for sorting and patterning practice. Or have students add them to the adorable volcano craft on page 13!

Stegosaurus and Tyrannosaurus rex Patterns

Use with "Little *Stegosaurus*" on page 287, "Meat Eater, Plant Eater" on page 288, and "Give a Roar!" on page 289.

TEC41041

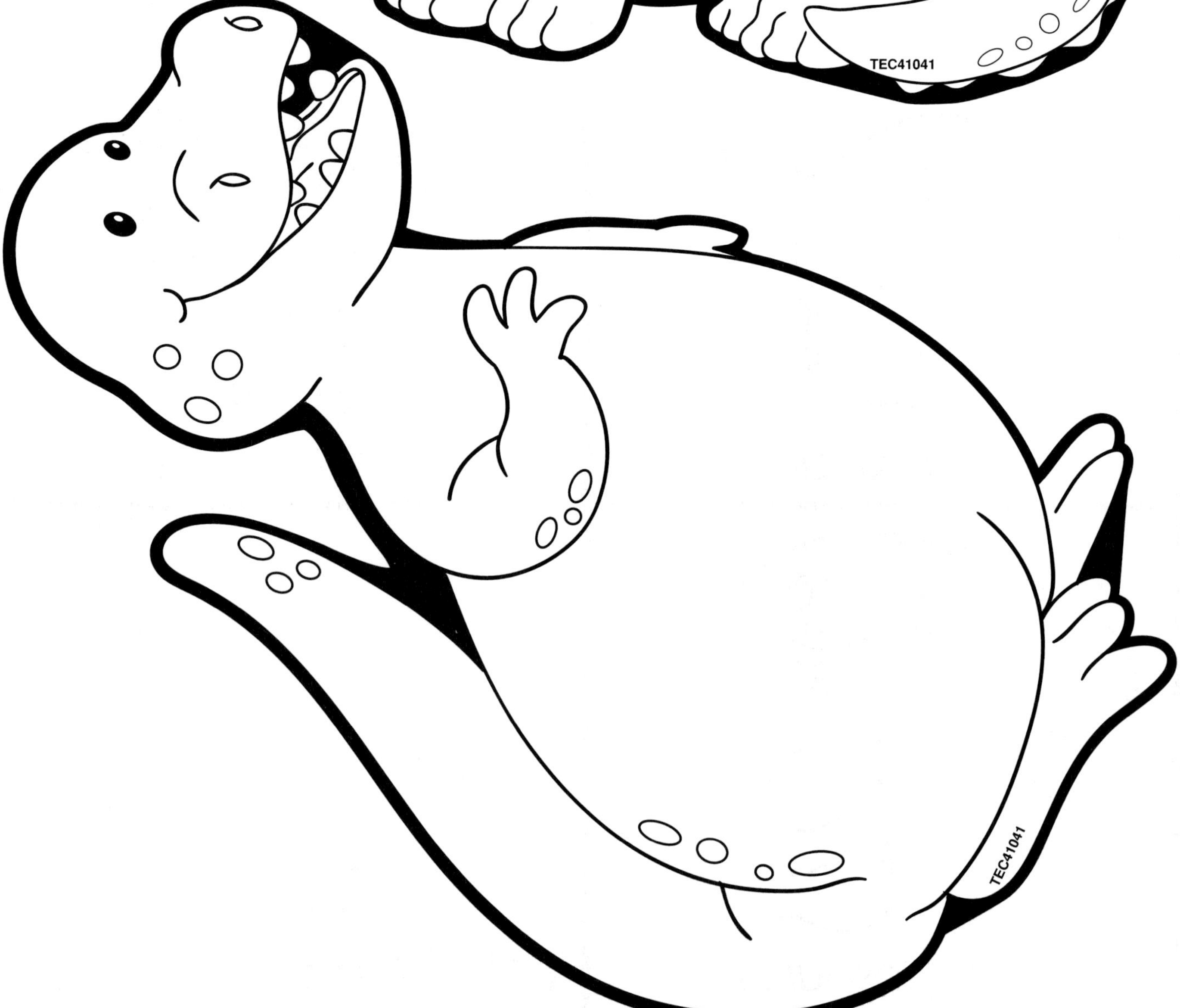

TEC41041

Triceratops
TEC41041

Pteranodon
TEC41041

Apatosaurus
TEC41041

Corythosaurus
TEC41041

Ankylosaurus
TEC41041

Plesiosaurus
TEC41041

Wonderful Wind

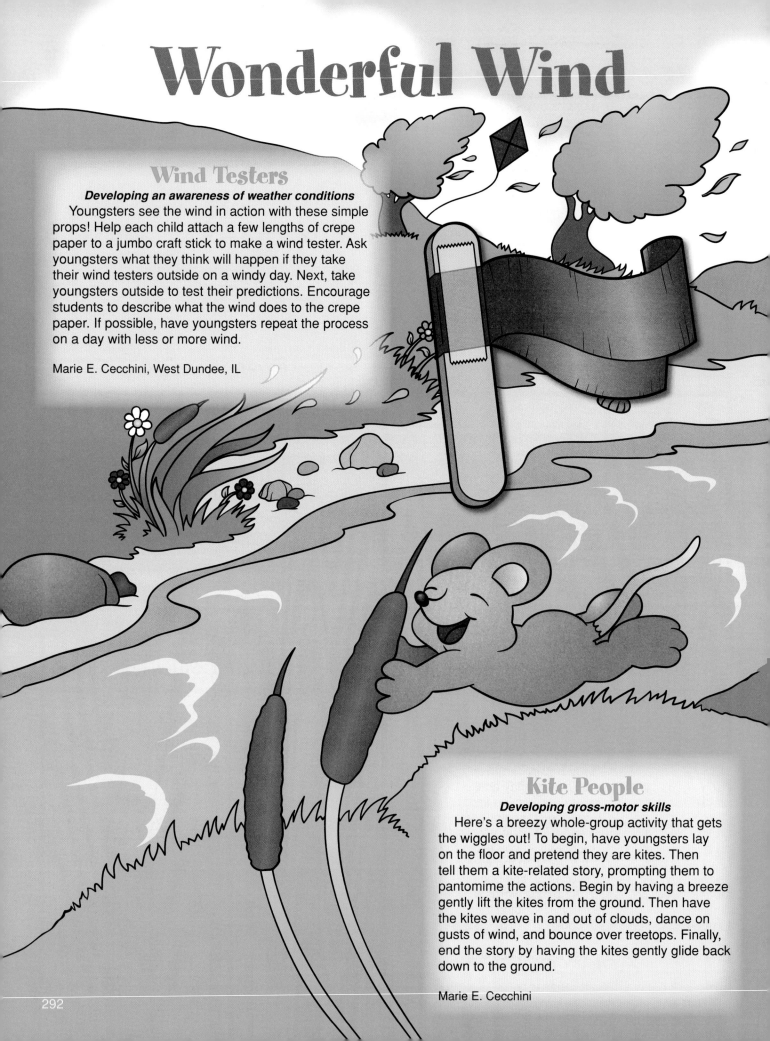

Wind Testers

Developing an awareness of weather conditions

Youngsters see the wind in action with these simple props! Help each child attach a few lengths of crepe paper to a jumbo craft stick to make a wind tester. Ask youngsters what they think will happen if they take their wind testers outside on a windy day. Next, take youngsters outside to test their predictions. Encourage students to describe what the wind does to the crepe paper. If possible, have youngsters repeat the process on a day with less or more wind.

Marie E. Cecchini, West Dundee, IL

Kite People

Developing gross-motor skills

Here's a breezy whole-group activity that gets the wiggles out! To begin, have youngsters lay on the floor and pretend they are kites. Then tell them a kite-related story, prompting them to pantomime the actions. Begin by having a breeze gently lift the kites from the ground. Then have the kites weave in and out of clouds, dance on gusts of wind, and bounce over treetops. Finally, end the story by having the kites gently glide back down to the ground.

Marie E. Cecchini

Will It Blow Away?

Predicting

Gather a variety of common classroom objects that may or may not blow away on a windy day. Place the objects on your floor along with a chart labeled as shown. Have youngsters predict which items will or will not take flight in the wind by placing them on the chart. Then take the objects outside on a windy day and place them on a flat surface. Have students observe the objects to determine whether their predictions were correct.

Jennifer Snyder, The Children's Garden, Easton, PA

Will Blow Away | Will Not Blow Away

Whoosh, Whoosh!

Identifying body parts

Give each youngster a blue crepe paper streamer to represent the wind. Then lead youngsters in singing the song shown, prompting them to wave their streamers across the appropriate body part.

(sung to the tune of "If You're Happy and You Know It")

Oh, the wind blows on my [knees], on my
 [knees]. Whoosh, whoosh!
Oh, the wind blows on my [knees], on my
 [knees]. Whoosh, whoosh!
Oh, the wind blows all around with a whooshing,
 whooshing sound.
Oh, the wind blows on my [knees], on my
 [knees]. Whoosh, whoosh!

Continue with the following: *back, tummy, elbows, head, ankles, feet, arms, legs*

Lisa Shaia, Bristol, CT

Play Like the Wind

Creating a story innovation

In the story *Like a Windy Day* by Frank and Devin Asch, a little girl imagines she can play as the wind plays: racing through the streets, waving flags, and lifting birds in the sky. Read the story aloud. Then grab your digital camera and take youngsters outside on a windy day. Have students help you take photographs of items that are moving with the wind. Then attach the photos to construction paper. Have students help you add to the pages words reminiscent of the words in the story. Then bind the pages together to make a class book.

Litsa Jackson, Covington Integrated Arts Academy
 Covington, TN
Carolynn Sidlauskas, Covert Elementary
 Covert, MI

Hat Thief
Reciting a rhyme

That sneaky wind has been known to steal a few hats! Color and cut out a copy of the cards on page 295. Attach a piece of Velcro fastener to the back of each card. Place the baker's hat card on your flannelboard and have students identify who would wear the hat. Then lead students in reciting the rhyme shown. Repeat the process with the remaining cards, changing the underlined word in the rhyme as appropriate.

"The wind took my hat—oh dear, oh my!
"The wind took my hat up into the sky.
"I need my hat," the [baker] said.
"I need my hat to cover my head!"

Candy Grzadziel, Elgin, IL

Windy Trees
Expressing oneself through art

To make this windy tree art, have a child draw a tree trunk on a sheet of construction paper. Then encourage him to drip diluted green paint on the paper. Have him blow through a straw in a consistent direction to move the paint. The result is a tree with leaves blown about on a windy day!

Essra Paddock, Shooting Stars Family Daycare, Warwick, NY

Wind Debris
Exploring the earth

Poke a hole near the edge of a large plastic lid and thread a piece of yarn through the hole to make a hanger. Then have youngsters help you spread petroleum jelly on both sides of the lid. Take students outside on a windy day and have them watch as you hang the lid from a tree. The next day, have youngsters help you retrieve the lid. Then encourage students to notice the dirt and other debris caught in the petroleum jelly. Prompt youngsters to suggest where the debris came from, encouraging them to conclude that on windy days dirt, sand, and other items are blown into the air.

C. Welwood, Learning Experience, Calgary, Alberta, Canada

TEC41041

What Did the Wind Blow?

296

Note to the teacher: Have each youngster cut pictures from magazines and attach them to her page. Then help her label each picture.

Sensational Seeds

What Will Grow?
Predicting, observing

Youngsters predict which items will grow with this simple science activity! Show youngsters a variety of small objects, including some seeds. Have students predict which items will grow when planted. Then encourage little ones to help you plant the items in labeled cups. Have youngsters water the items and then place the cups in a sunny window. Direct students to observe the cups for the next few weeks and then evaluate their predictions.

Marie E. Cecchini
West Dundee, IL

Swirling Seeds
Investigating living things

This unique discovery bottle has a seed-themed twist! Place basil seeds in an empty plastic bottle. Then fill the bottle with water and tape or hot glue the lid in place. Put the bottle in a sunny window. During center time, encourage students to shake and swirl the bottle, watching the seeds move. Then have them return the bottle to the window. After several days, the seeds will begin to sprout!

Erin McGinness
Great New Beginnings
Bear, DE

Basil

Seeds

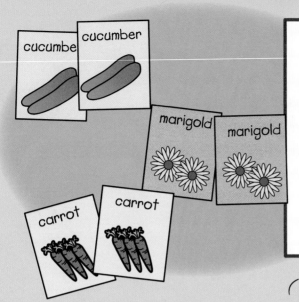

Packet Match
Matching

Gather pairs of empty seed packets. (Youngsters' parents may have green thumbs! Consider sending a note home to request packets.) Laminate the packets and place them in a center. A youngster spreads the packets out so they are faceup. Then he matches the pairs of packets.

Sue Reppert
Widening World Preschool
Mentor, OH

A Seed Song
Participating in a song

Lead youngsters in singing the song shown. When they are comfortable with the words and tune, give each youngster a seed shaker (beans in a plastic bottle). Prompt students to shake the instruments as they sing the song. Then collect the seed shakers for safekeeping.

(sung to the tune of "Twinkle, Twinkle, Little Star")

First you dig a little hole.
Then you drop the seeds in there.
Cover them with lots of dirt.
Give them water, sun, and care.
Now the seeds will start to sprout—
Flowers blooming all about.

Alda Martin
A Better Choice for Children
Charlotte, NC

From Seed to Sprout
Developing fine-motor skills

To prepare for this adorable and simple craft, fold a 6" x 18" piece of construction paper in half lengthwise for each youngster. After a planting activity, have each child unfold the paper and arrange it horizontally on a table. Then encourage him to paint the area below the fold line brown. Have him sprinkle glitter (seeds) on the wet paint. When the plants from your class project have sprouted, help students paint their fingers green and make prints (sprouts) above the fold line as shown.

Esther Campbell, Newfane ABCD, Newfane, NY

Five Little Seeds
Recognizing ordinal numbers

Make five seed cutouts and draw a face on each seed. Attach a piece of tape to the back of each seed and attach the seeds to your board. Then lead youngsters in performing the rhyme below, gesturing to each seed when appropriate.

Five little seeds buried in the ground;
The first one said, "When's the sun coming round?"
The second one said, "I really need a drink!"
The third one said, "I feel some rain, I think!"
The fourth one said, "I'm so cozy in my bed."
The fifth one said, "Wake up, you sleepyhead!"
The rain came down and the sun came out,
And those five little seeds—they started to sprout.

Julie McCray
Little Beavers Preschool
Corry, PA

Beans are seeds.

I ___like___ beans.

1

Peas are seeds.

I ___do not like___ peas.

2

Corn kernels are seeds.

I ___like___ corn.

3

Peanuts are seeds.

I ___like___ peanuts.

4

We Eat Seeds!
Developing print awareness

Give each child a copy of pages 301 and 302. Encourage each student to color her pages. Then have her make colorful fingerprints on the pages so they resemble the seeds described. Read the pages aloud and have the child share whether she enjoys eating each type of seed. Write "like" or "do not like" in the blanks. Cut out the pages and stack them in order behind a cover titled "We Eat Seeds!" Then bind the pages as desired.

Check This Out!
When Beth Lemke of Highland Family Center Headstart, Columbia Heights, MN, does planting projects with her youngsters, she helps them glue one of each type of seed to a separate craft stick. Then a child pushes each stick into the soil to use as a marker. The project is more meaningful because the students can refer to the seed as they watch the plant grow!

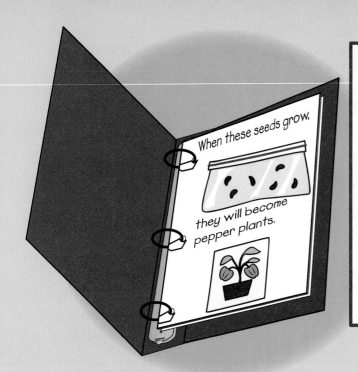

Seeds and Plants
Developing an independent interest in books
To help students become familiar with the appearance of seeds and the corresponding plants, put together this adorable seed book! For each page in the book, attach a picture of a plant and a snack-size resealable plastic bag containing the corresponding seeds. (Seal the top of the plastic bag with tape.) Add text similar to that shown. Place the resulting book at a center. Youngsters are sure to enjoy looking at the seeds and their matching plants.

Tanya Napier
Adventures in Learning
Tustin, CA

What's Inside?
Investigating living things
Place lima beans between layers of wet paper towels and seal them in a plastic bag overnight. Remove the beans the next day. Then gather a small group of youngsters and give each child a bean. Explain that beans are seeds. Then help little ones use a toothpick or tweezers to remove the thin outer layer and separate the halves of the bean. Once the bean is divided, youngsters can see the tiny plant inside. Prompt youngsters to notice the tiny plant and observe it with a magnifying glass.

Marie E. Cecchini
West Dundee, IL

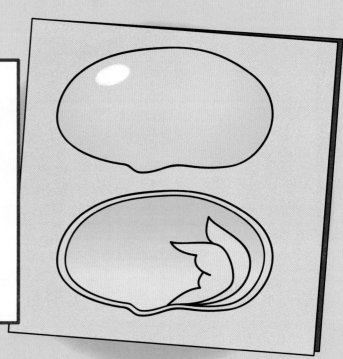

Spinning Seeds
Developing gross-motor skills
Collect seeds from a maple tree and allow them to dry out. Then give each child a seed. Encourage him to toss it into the air and then watch it whirl to the ground. Next, have students pretend to be maple seeds. Tell youngsters a story about the seeds, encouraging them to pantomime the actions in the story. Begin by having a breeze blow a seed from a tree. The seed twirls to the ground. Then the seed sprouts and grows into a new maple tree, which makes more little seeds. Repeat the story several times in a row to help youngsters understand the plant's life cycle.

Grace Gafford, Creative Learning Center, Smyrna, TN

Peas are seeds.

_____ peas.

2

Beans are seeds.

_____ beans.

1

Peanuts are seeds.

I _____ peanuts.

4

Corn kernels are seeds.

I _____ corn.

3

It's Easy to Be Green!

April 22 is Earth Day! Celebrate this important day with a selection of activities chosen to help youngsters appreciate the natural world and take care of Mother Earth.

Recycling Detectives
Developing visual discrimination

Help youngsters identify recyclable materials with this fun activity! Gather a variety of clean recyclable containers and place them in your circle-time area. Invite each youngster to pick up a container and search for the triangular recycling symbol. When he finds it, encourage him to bring the container to you and show you the symbol. Then give the youngster a stamp on his hand. Have him place the container back in the circle-time area and repeat the process with a new container. Youngsters are sure to love hunting for the symbols and collecting stamps!

Karla Broad, Our Savior Preschool, Naples, FL

Water Litter
Promoting Earth-friendly habits

To show youngsters what litter can do to clean water, partially fill a large plastic jug with water. Then have youngsters watch as you place trash in the water and secure the jug's lid. Have students observe the jug for several days, noting that the water becomes cloudy and dirty. Ask youngsters whether fish, frogs, and other animals could live in the dirty water, leading them to conclude that dumping trash in the water can be harmful to wildlife.

Marie E. Cecchini, West Dundee, FL

Earth-Friendly Art
Developing artistic expression

Youngsters reuse objects to create this masterpiece of modern art! For each child, gather a black foam vegetable tray. Encourage each youngster to paint several pieces of cardboard tube. (Metallic paint looks particularly striking.) Hot-glue each child's painted tubes to his tray. Then prompt each youngster to drizzle glue over the tubes and sprinkle glitter over the wet glue.

Jacqueline Higgins, Eastminster Presbyterian Preschool
Indialantic, FL

Reduce, Reuse, Recycle
Participating in a song

Lead youngsters in singing the song below. If desired, encourage students to tap two cardboard tubes against each other to lend percussion to the sing-along!

(sung to the tune of "For He's a Jolly Good Fellow")

Reduce, reuse, recycle.
Reduce, reuse, recycle.
Reduce, reuse, recycle.
Be kind to Mother Earth.
Be kind to Mother Earth.
Be kind to Mother Earth.
(Repeat the first four lines.)

Dotty Eaton, Oak Park/River Forest Day Nursery, Oak Park, IL

Be Kind
Developing recall skills

Read aloud *Each Living Thing* by Joanne Ryder. This gorgeously illustrated book uses simple text to encourage youngsters to observe living things, respect them, and let them be. After the read-aloud, give each child a copy of page 306 and a crayon. Guide students to focus on one animal on the page at a time and ask them whether the animal was shown in the story. Look back at the book's illustrations when necessary. Have each child circle the animals that were found in the story. Then encourage students to identify the remaining animals and color the page as desired.

Pleasing Plants
Investigating living things

This simple activity will make your classroom look green indeed! Ask parents to donate cuttings of house-plants. Then have students help you place the cuttings in containers of water and put the containers near a window. Encourage students to notice that some cuttings grow roots and others do not. After several weeks, have students help plant the cuttings that have grown roots.

Marie E. Cecchini, West Dundee, IL

Go Green!
Participating in a song

Before youngsters sing this song, explain that a person who is "green" does things to help the earth.

(sung to the tune of "If You're Happy and You Know It")

Do you know what it means to be green?   *Clap twice.*
Do you know what it means to be green?   *Clap twice.*
[To be green, you have to care about the ocean and the air.]
Do you know what it means to be green?   *Clap twice.*

Continue with the following:
To be green, I will choose to reduce and reuse.
I'll recycle every day, and the earth will shout, "Hooray!"

Jermain Lawrie, Kathleen E. Goodwin Elementary, Old Saybrook, CT

A Messy Lake!
Developing eye-hand coordination

Place a large lake cutout on the floor in a center. Attach magnets to several pieces of clean litter. Place the litter on the lake along with several fish cutouts. Transform a dowel rod or yardstick into a fishing pole by tying string to it. Then tie a large washer to the end of the string. A youngster maneuvers the fishing pole to remove the litter from the lake.

Susan Pufall, Red Cliff Early Childhood Center, Bayfield, WI

Take Care of Living Things

Name _____

306

©The Mailbox® · TEC41042 · April/May 2009

Note to the teacher: Use with "Be Kind" on page 304.

Playful Pirates!

Ahoy, mateys! This selection of pirate– and treasure–themed ideas is sure to please pirates and landlubbers alike!

Gather a Crew

Developing phonological awareness

Here's an entertaining pirate-themed twist on the game I Spy! If desired, don a pirate hat and an eye patch. Then explain that you are the captain of a pirate ship and need a crew. Use a large cardboard tube (spyglass) to scan your youngsters. Say, "I spy pirates whose names begin with [/b/]." Then prompt students whose names begin with /b/ to "board" the ship and stand next to you. Repeat the process until all your youngsters have come aboard and you have a full crew. Then "sail" with your little ones around the room!

Janet Boyce, Cokato, MN

Dig Up the Treasure!

Making sets

To prepare for this activity, place treasure chest cutouts (see page 311 for a pattern) near your sand table. For each treasure chest, bury five pieces of treasure in the sand. You may consider using lengths of gold pipecleaners, pieces of junk jewelry, silver rickrack, and jumbo plastic coins. Provide plastic shovels and other digging tools. Youngsters dig the pieces of treasure from the sand table, inspect them, and then place five pieces on each treasure chest.

Janet Boyce

Paper Plate Pirate
Developing fine-motor skills

To make this adorable pirate craft, paint a paper plate with skin tone tempera paint. When the paint is dry, glue a semicircle of fabric to the plate. Next, glue a piece of black craft foam below the fabric so it resembles an eye patch. Use a permanent marker to add details. Then punch holes in opposite sides of the plate. Attach a metal ring to one hole. Thread a strip of fabric through the remaining hole and knot it in place. This little pirate is too cute!

Sue Fleischmann, Sussex, WI

Over the Waves!
Counting

This action rhyme is a real treasure! Have students perform the rhyme five times, increasing the number by one each time and changing the pronouns from *his* and *he* to *their* and *they* as needed.

Over the waves,	*Pretend to row a boat.*
With his boat and his oar,	*Continue rowing.*
[One] little pirate came to shore.	*Hold up [one] finger.*
He buried his treasure deep in the sand,	*Pretend to dig.*
Got back in his boat, and left the land.	*Place finger(s) on cupped hand (boat).*

LeeAnn Collins, Sunshine House Preschool, Lansing, MI

What's in the Box?
Predicting book events

Make a copy of the treasure chest on page 311, cut it out, and attach it to a sheet of chart paper. Obtain a copy of *This Little Pirate* by Philemon Sturges. This adorable story, fashioned after the traditional rhyme "This Little Piggy," tells the tale of two bands of pirate pigs that squabble over a box on an island. Read aloud the story, stopping when the pirates are about to open the box. Then ask youngsters what they think is in the box and write their predictions around the treasure chest. Finally, finish the story and have students revisit their predictions.

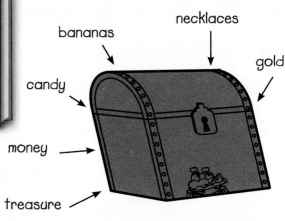

necklaces

bananas

gold

candy

money

treasure

X Marks the Spot
Writing letter X
Consider adding this supersimple activity to a pirate-themed dramatic-play area! Gather several road maps and place them at a center along with a variety of writing utensils. A youngster draws Xs on the map to indicate where he'll find treasure.

Suzanne Foote, East Ithaca Preschool, Ithaca, NY

Pirate Bounty
Following directions
Collect the following ingredients for this tasty snack mix: mini chocolate sandwich cookies (eye patches), thin pretzel sticks (wooden legs), Mini Ritz crackers (gold coins), and sea-themed gummy candies. Place each ingredient in a separate bowl and place a large spoon in each bowl. Prompt each student to carefully place one spoonful of each ingredient in a resealable plastic bag. Then have your little pirates nibble on their snacks.

Nancy Foss, Wee Care, Galion, OH

Check This Out!
Janna Meister of Parkwood Weekday Early Education Center, Jacksonville, Florida, has come up with a pirate-themed take on a fishing game! She hot-glues a magnet to a plastic hook hand (found at costume and party supply stores). Then she has a student use the hook to pick up juice lids (gold) labeled with letters and numbers for the child to identify. What a fun and unique classroom prop!

Walk the Plank!
Developing gross-motor skills

Your little pirates will love practicing balance and coordination with this activity! Cut a wide strip of wood grain decorative Con-Tact covering. Then attach it to your floor so it resembles a wooden plank. Place a plastic hoop at one end of the plank. Then scatter sea creature cutouts (see pages 260 and 312) around the plank. A youngster walks along the plank and then jumps into the hoop. Watch out for that octopus!

Janet Boyce, Cokato, MN

So Many Feelings!
Exploring emotions

Lead youngsters in singing this song and pantomiming each appropriate emotion.

(sung to the tune of "If You're Happy and You Know It")

I'm a very [scary] pirate on my ship. Argh! Argh!
I'm a very [scary] pirate on my ship. Argh! Argh!
I will sail to each new place
With this [scary] looking face!
I'm a very [scary] pirate on my ship. Argh! Argh!

Continue with: *silly, happy, angry, weepy*

LeeAnn Collins, Sunshine House Preschool, Lansing, MI

A Spiffy Hat
Writing

For each child, make two cutouts of the hat shape shown. Have her use a white crayon to decorate the cutouts. After you staple the cutouts together, encourage her to glue a cotton ball and two cotton swabs, as shown, to the hat. When the glue is dry, take a close-up photo of each youngster wearing her hat. Ask her what she would do if she were a pirate. Then write her words in a speech bubble cutout and display it with her trimmed photo. If desired, embellish the display with foil coins and sea critters (see pages 260 and 312).

Janet Boyce

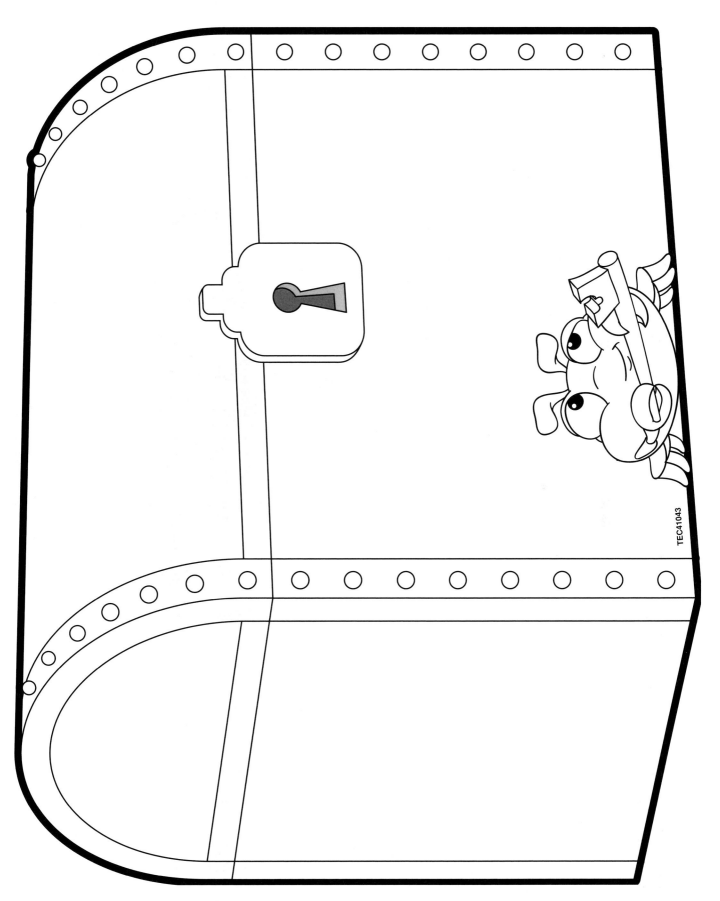

TEC41043

TEC41043

Index